PRAISE FOR
VALUABLE CONTENT MARKETING

"Valuable content is the focus of all successful marketing today. In our always-wired new commercial world, buyers want access to all information, and they'll get it – if not from you, then from your competitor. They don't want positioning or testimonials – they want to sample your wares themselves. The successful firm practices 21st century samples selling by providing valuable content, knowing that buyers prefer sellers who are willing to show what they know. This book tells you why this is true, and how to play in the new game." **Charles H Green, author of** *The Trusted Advisor*

"Sonja and Sharon provide great insights on the dynamic practice of content marketing. Their book is full of commercial arguments showing why content marketing is the backbone of revenue growth, and practical tips on how to create a sustainable and effective content strategy. The illustrations are cool too." **Paul Wilson, Chief Marketing Officer, Fortune 500 SunGard**

"This is the clearest, most complete, and easiest to understand book available on how to do content marketing the right way. If you follow their formula you will succeed. *Valuable Content Marketing* is just that... valuable! It is destined to be a modern marketing classic. Buy this book before your competitors do or you will be sorry!" **Lee Frederikson, managing partner at Hinge Marketing, author of** *Spiralling Up*

"If you're not mad, read this book. You would be mad to do business with someone you didn't trust, but in a world of seemingly endless choices, how do people know they can trust you? Being honest and open about what you can do to help them is a pretty good start. But how do you communicate that if you're not in front of them? Having read this immensely helpful book, I now know it is by creating valuable content: something interesting and valuable you can publish online; content that educates, helps or inspires; content appreciated by the reader. This book shows you how with vivid clarity."
    Stephen King, author of *Finance on a Beermat*, www.f-works.co.uk

"This is the best book available about valuable content marketing. Practical, a delight to read and full of valuable content, it will be on the reading list for all my clients." **David Tovey, Author of** *Principled Selling*

"In the 21st century post-advertising apocalypse – we don't want to be shouted at or sold to. We want to be listened to and helped – and this book, very clearly, explains how this can work for you." **Robin Kermode, author of** *The Authentic Speaker, Zone2 The Art of Communication*

"This book is a fantastic look into the thinking behind modern marketing. Sonja and Sharon present the theory, back it up with examples of how – and why – it works and then provide "take action" ideas to help their readers with its implementation. Backed up with further insight from successful adopters, the information in this book has been very useful to me as I start out in business myself. Reading it felt like a chat over coffee – friendly, useful and engaging. Just the way modern marketing should be."

Nick Rapson, IT Services

"Creating truly valuable content is part skill, part science and part mysterious martial art! Get it right and you quickly resonate with your audience; get it wrong and your brand can be toast. Luckily Sharon and Sonja are the perfect combination of teachers, scientists and experts and so their book is simply a must read. For beginners, it provides a step by step guide to success and for the more experienced it contains perfect reminders on what works and what doesn't. Great work!" **Richard Dennys, Chief Marketing Officer, Qype**

"There is a new vernacular in what successful business developers do. They explore, help and seek to assist their client in adding value to their organization. They always look to share something new and they co-develop solutions. Most importantly this differentiation is scalable, can transcend all activity and is sustainable at individual and organizational level. The *Valuable Content Marketing* book demonstrates that this is a great model for success and that the move to trusted adviser is achievable for all who choose to engage. Of course, you can continue to push to the many in the hope that you may attract a few. I know what I prefer."

Emma Price, Director of Business Development, Bond Pearce LLP

"Every modern day sales person, marketing professional and business entrepreneur that is worth their salt and wants to thrive in today's ever changing market needs to read this book! And with this succinct, practical and engaging guide to valuable content there's every incentive to start embracing and implementing a valuable content approach with immediate effect and realising the benefits of increased market engagement. Highly recommended." **Ryan James, Playmaker Services**

VALUABLE
CONTENT
MARKETING

Don't ever try to sell me on anything.
Give me ALL the information
and I'll make my own decision.
RAPPER KANYE WEST IN A TWEET

VALUABLE
CONTENT
MARKETING

WHY QUALITY CONTENT IS KEY TO BUSINESS SUCCESS

SONJA JEFFERSON & SHARON TANTON

KoganPage

LONDON PHILADELPHIA NEW DELHI

Publisher's note

Every possible effort has been made to ensure that the information contained in this book is accurate at the time of going to press, and the publishers and authors cannot accept responsibility for any errors or omissions, however caused. No responsibility for loss or damage occasioned to any person acting, or refraining from action, as a result of the material in this publication can be accepted by the editor, the publisher or either of the authors.

First published in Great Britain and the United States in 2013 by Kogan Page Limited

120 Pentonville Road
London N1 9JN
United Kingdom
www.koganpage.com

1518 Walnut Street, Suite 1100
Philadelphia PA 19102
USA

4737/23 Ansari Road
Daryaganj
New Delhi 110002
India

© Sonja Jefferson and Sharon Tanton, 2013
Illustrations © Lizzie Everard, 2012

ISBN   978 0 7494 6580 3
E-ISBN 978 0 7494 6581 0

British Library Cataloguing-in-Publication Data

A CIP record for this book is available from the British Library.

Library of Congress Cataloging-in-Publication Data

Jefferson, Sonja.
  Valuable content marketing : how to make quality content the key to your business success / Sonja Jefferson, Sharon Tanton.
     p. cm.
  Includes index.
  ISBN 978-0-7494-6580-3 – ISBN 978-0-7494-6581-0   1. Marketing.   2. Internet marketing.
3. Customer relations.   I. Tanton, Sharon.   II. Title.
  HF5415.J42 2012
  658.8–dc23
                                                                                   2012020101

Typeset by Graphicraft Limited, Hong Kong
Printed and bound in India by Replika Press Pvt Ltd

CONTENTS

ABOUT THE AUTHORS

Sonja Jefferson is a writer, consultant and thought leader in the art of high quality content generation for sales results.

Sonja's early career in various business-to-business sales positions, from telemarketing to sales management, taught her at ground level why some sales approaches worked whilst others fell short. An early adopter of blogging as a business development tool, Sonja proved that companies of all sizes and remits could attract the interest of their target audiences through generously sharing useful content – creating unprecedented levels of interest and engagement compared to traditional, self-oriented marketing campaigns.

As the founder of UK marketing communications firm Valuable Content and a director of The Principled Group Ltd Sonja now helps owners of professional service businesses to place high quality content at the heart of their marketing. She advises on how to get the best out of digital marketing methods, creates high-performing websites and quality business books – all based on the valuable content principles.

Referred to by clients as the marketer who thinks like a sales person, Sonja understands the high-pressured demands of sales and the solution which is proving to be the future of marketing.

She lives in Bristol with her young family, spending her free time travelling to West Country beaches in her camper van where she loves to surf, swim and run.

www.valuablecontent.co.uk

Sharon Tanton is a specialist copywriter and content creator who uses her fine-tuned wordsmith skills to help businesses communicate their message through original, creative content.

Having worked on features at the BBC's *Radio Times* magazine, on various award-winning social history documentaries and as an English teacher, Sharon cultivated a passion and talent for creating the narrative which could bring a business's marketing to life. Sharon went on to create content for high-profile internal staff publications and corporate communications for organizations such as Barclays, where she honed the ability to engage both company directors and staff alike.

As the creative director at Valuable Content, Sharon brings the human touch to businesses by create compelling and engaging messages and content campaigns. With a passion for literature and having written a novel, Sharon is known to many industry colleagues as the writer who makes commercial marketing more lovable.

Sharon lives in Bristol with partner Bill, five of their eight children and her dog Bella. She loves photography, gardening and walking.

www.valuablecontent.co.uk

INTRODUCTION
WHY YOU NEED THIS BOOK

Once upon a time selling seemed simpler. You held all the cards. A brochure, a sales team, some adverts and you were away. If people wanted to know more you could drop a brochure in the post, and have one of your sales team follow up with a call next week. Now, people are able to research online, and ask the opinions of thousands in minutes. Your products and services need to be found quickly and stand up to scrutiny. And, that's where marketing with valuable content matters.

For today's savvy, cynical, connected buyers, old-style marketing no longer works. No one will wait three days for the information they want to drop on to the doormat. We all expect answers NOW. And we will not stand for sales spiel either. '*Buy this, it's great*' won't cut it. You need to inform, entertain, and most of all, help people through to a purchase.

In our online world, getting your web strategy and 'content' right has never been more important, but what content do you share? Producing a quantity of any old content isn't the answer. It is only high quality, *valuable* content that is trusted, read and shared. By valuable content we mean information that is genuinely useful, relevant, informative or entertaining. Whether it is helpful pages on your websites, articles on your blog, social media updates, newsletters, video or books like this, valuable content is smart marketing communication that gets results. If you regularly share this type of information you will draw people to your business – the company that inspires, understands and offers clear answers is the obvious place to turn when the time comes to buy.

Valuable content is magnetic. It will draw people to your business.

able content is a very different approach from the majority of the ou see. Most businesses and websites focus on pushing dull, sales messages that are ignored rather than welcomed as some- ιe. If you want success from your marketing stop 'selling' and start helping instead. We will show you how to stand out from the crowd by getting your content just right.

Like many good ideas, marketing with valuable content is very simple. It means seeing your business from your customers' point of view – offering answers, developing relationships, being there when they need you, putting your own agenda aside. It's the smart, natural approach to winning business, one that we have used to successfully grow our own company and many client companies too. Marketing the valuable way is a far cry from the unrewarding drudgery of cold calling or blanket-bomb direct mail campaigns. If you continually share information that people actually value, clients and customers will *choose* to come to you.

If you are the kind of person who would rather attract business than chase business then Valuable Content Marketing *is for you.*

What you will learn in this book

This book tells you all you need to know to focus your marketing efforts on creating really valuable content – on and off the web – for fantastic business results. We want to bring content to the surface in your organization – so it becomes something you proactively use to generate leads and sales.

By the end of the book you will have the confidence to create and distribute the kind of information that your customers find, appreciate, act on and willingly share. You will learn:

- why creating and sharing valuable content is so effective today;
- how to get the best out of new marketing tools at your disposal – blogging, social media, video, e-books, email marketing;
- how to make your website valuable;
- how to distribute your valuable content so it reaches the people who buy your products or services;

- how salespeople can use valuable content to open doors for better sales conversations;
- a practical, step-by-step content marketing strategy for your business;
- how to uncover your organization's hidden store of valuable content;
- how to write the type of content that people want to find and share.

We'll answer the big three questions many people have around marketing with content:

1 Why should I give knowledge away for free?
2 How can I find the time?
3 What on earth can I write about?

Who this book is for

If you believe in your business and want to know how to get your message across then this book is for you. Whether you are a business owner, executive or seasoned sales and marketing professional you'll find information, tips and stories to inspire you from companies large and small.

The approach we set out here is particularly relevant for professional businesses with big growth ambitions and modest marketing budgets, for marketing with valuable content is a very powerful and cost-effective route to sales success.

If you are starting a business, thinking about creating a new website, blog, social media feed or just want better sales results from your marketing efforts this book will show you the way.

Our story

Writing this book came as a result of what we have seen happening in business over the last decade. We have been creating valuable, lead-generating marketing strategies, websites and books for professional firms in the UK, and sharing what we have learned on our blogs. We started a newsletter, and have spread our content far and wide through various social media channels, and on industry websites. It has brought in a lot of business for us without ever having to chase people for work, and the strategy has transformed many client businesses too. We have proved that if you make your marketing valuable to those you want to do business with they will reward you with their business and loyalty. It's a simple approach that gets results.

Yet, companies marketing this way are still in the minority. Although what has become known as 'content marketing' is gaining in popularity, the majority of businesses haven't caught up. We still see businesses trying to market themselves with websites that just aren't up to the job. Many of these are great companies run by bright, intelligent experts who know their stuff but aren't connecting with their customers – and are losing out as a result. They are missing a trick with their marketing and we want to fix this.

Writing blogs, engaging in social media, and giving away valuable information to build your business is uncharted water for many firms. Combining Sonja's professional sales and business development background with Sharon's marketing and copywriting expertise has unearthed a really useful seam of 'what to write' and 'how to write it'. It is that practical hands on approach that we want to share with you in this book.

Our mission is to rid the world of websites that don't work, to inspire business owners to get to grips with sharing their knowledge on the web and off, and in doing so, to connect with their customers and build better, stronger businesses.

How to use this book

The book is in three parts:

- Chapters 1 to 3 explain the why – why valuable content is so crucial today.
- Chapters 4 to 12 explain the what – the tools at your disposal and how to make them valuable.
- Chapters 13 to 14 explain the how – practical steps for content marketing success.

You'll find action points to follow at the end of each chapter and extra resources and templates to assist you at the back of the book. You'll find a quick assessment in the Resources section at the end of the book to help you check how valuable your content is now. Start at the beginning and read on from there.

There are more free resources, articles and e-books on the Valuable Content website, blog and social media feeds **www.valuablecontent.co.uk**.

The secret to effective marketing is simple: make yourself useful and share information that your buyers genuinely value, even look forward to. Isn't it time your business learned how to create some really valuable content?

Let's get started.

PART ONE
WHY VALUABLE CONTENT?

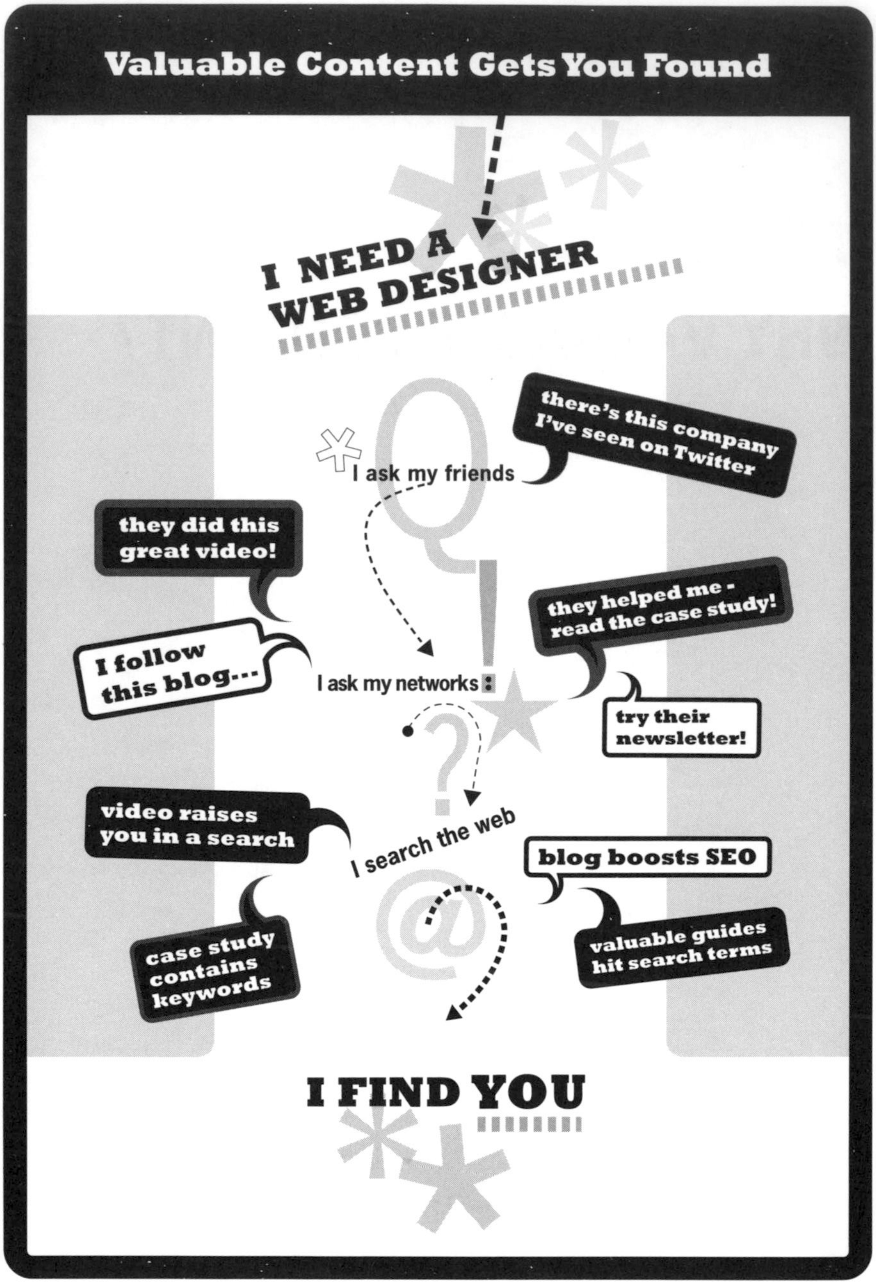
Valuable Content Gets You Found
I NEED A WEB DESIGNER
I ask my friends
there's this company I've seen on Twitter
they did this great video!
I follow this blog...
I ask my networks
they helped me - read the case study!
try their newsletter!
video raises you in a search
I search the web
blog boosts SEO
case study contains keywords
valuable guides hit search terms
I FIND YOU

CHAPTER 1
MARKETING HAS CHANGED. HAVE YOU?

Search engines, blogs and other Internet trends have fundamentally transformed the way people and businesses purchase products (and services), but most small businesses still use out-dated, inefficient marketing methods – like print advertising, telemarketing and trade shows – that people increasingly find intrusive and screen out.

Brian Halligan, CEO of Hubspot and author of
Inbound Marketing **www.hubspot.com @hubspot**

In this chapter:

- The business development challenge.
- How successful businesses are marketing themselves today.
- What are these companies doing right?
- The three factors transforming buyer behaviour.
- The new buyer mentality.
- Buyers prefer valuable content.

Learn why some companies are winning the business development challenge, even in a tough market. We look at the three trends influencing buyer behaviour today and explain why people prefer valuable content.

The business development challenge

Business development has always been one of the toughest challenges facing any company. Business owners and professionals in every marketing and sales department face the same concerns:

How do I find new clients? How can I differentiate myself/my organization from the competition? How can I get more referrals and cross-sell more effectively? How can I smooth out the boom and bust lumps in my sales cycle?

It's an age-old dilemma that for many seems to be getting tougher. Tried and tested activities for getting customer attention are just not working like they once did:

- Advertising rarely gets enough response to justify the considerable costs.
- The specialist press you once relied on for coverage has at best shrunk and at worst completely disappeared.
- In a tough, competitive market your old network isn't delivering all the leads you need to keep ahead.
- The response to cold calling and mass email campaigns is way, way down.

In 2006, according to research by Hot to Trot Marketing, it took only six calls from a telemarketing firm to make one contact; in 2010 this had rocketed to 41! In 2012 it is tougher still.

Recent research by digital news site Mashable finds that 44 per cent of direct mail is never opened (that's a waste of time, postage and paper); 86 per cent of people skip through television commercials; 84 per cent of 25- to 34-year-olds have clicked out of a website because of an 'irrelevant or intrusive ad'. Traditional advertising messages just aren't getting through.

As of February 2012, over 17 million UK phone numbers were registered with the Telephone Preference Service – demonstrating a huge swathe of the population that doesn't want to receive sales calls.

It no longer makes economic sense to send an advertising message to the many in the hopes of persuading a few.

M Lawrence Light – former Chief Marketing Officer of McDonalds

Yet many firms are continuing with the same promotional techniques they've always used. If you are relying on these methods to generate leads for your business it may seem as if your customers and clients aren't listening any more. You are expert in what you do and know that there are buyers out there who would really benefit from your services or products. How on earth do you get their attention?

It's enough to put some off marketing all together. For those who need to promote their businesses a traditional approach to marketing can feel unnatural, a bit manipulative, but mainly downright frustrating when you waste money and effort on 'techniques' that just don't work.

How successful businesses are marketing themselves today

Some companies are winning, even in a tough market. They are consistently getting a stream of good leads for their business – from their websites and from social media too. Their networks are expanding rapidly and delivering warm referrals that are easy to convert. They are doing all this without resorting to cold calling, expensive advertising or mass email blasts. In fact, clients and customers are calling THEM. To top it off, they say that they enjoy marketing too!

Businesses who are winning with their marketing (by sector):

Independent professionals

Mel Lester generates 70 per cent of new consulting business through his marketing activity. Mel shares his knowledge generously with the architecture and engineering community he serves via his website, blog, Twitter feed and monthly newsletter. **www.bizedge.biz**

Web designer Iain Claridge, whose beautiful and inspirational design blog lands him work all over the world, most notably with NASA. **www.iainclaridge.co.uk**

Marketing strategist Bryony Thomas, who has generated £800,000 worth of business in three years through sharing valuable marketing tips online for her small business clients. **www.bryonythomas.com**

Professional firms

Law firm Inksters buck their profession's trend of reticence over online market-ing and social media. Their expertise shines through the valuable content they share on Twitter, their niche websites and videos, drawing in 20 per cent of new leads straight from the web and bolstering personal recommendations too. **www.inksters.com**

Tensile fabric specialists Base Structures' valuable new website and content marketing programme has helped them to beat the recession. They have seen the value of order enquiries triple as a result. **www.basestructures.com**

The Payroll Services Centre packed their new website with helpful content, including a resources section, jargon buster, blog, downloads, newsletter and social media feeds. In just two months their Google ranking soared. Their content-focused marketing strategy draws in over 60 inbound leads a month. **www.payroll-services-centre.co.uk**

Creative companies

Start-up design studio Yoke, just six weeks after launch, had all the clients they could handle and more waiting in the wings thanks to their stunning, content-rich website, compelling proposition and Twitter relationships. **thisisyoke.com**

Business to consumer

Endurancelife: a UK endurance sports business went from 0 to 15,000 Facebook fans in a year because of the value of the content they share, doubling the participants at their events and turning them into a global lifestyle brand. **www.endurancelife.co.uk**

Major businesses

Intel Corporation focuses on creating valuable content for each of its different communities. Their blogs, social media feeds, video and even processor 'art' give the company a human face and expand the reach of their messages. **scoop.intel.com**

Even Coca-Cola, long wedded to creative advertising, announced in 2012 that it was switching its focus to sharing excellent content to grow the business. **www.coca-cola.co.uk**

And us!

And our company, Valuable Content Ltd, who receive enough inbound leads that we can pick and choose who we work for without ever having to hunt for new clients. **www.valuablecontent.co.uk**

[You'll find case studies for these and more businesses throughout the book.]

What are these companies doing right?

All are benefiting from a better way to generate business – more effective, more rewarding and far more comfortable than continually pushing at a door marked 'closed'. They focus on making their marketing valuable to their particular customers and their generosity is getting results:

- **Marketing online.** They are actively marketing online, opening up their marketing to the generosity of the Internet and they are getting their online strategies right.

- **With *valuable* content.** Their marketing and web strategy centres on continuously creating and sharing valuable content, not overt sales messages. Their websites are not just flat online brochures; they are filled with helpful information for their types of customers.

- **Clear message.** They are crystal clear on what they do and who their customers are. Those that get the best results have a clear understanding of who they do business with and what makes their customers or clients tick. They create relevant content just for them.

- **They are generous.** They fully understand the old adage that if you give you will get. They freely give away valuable information that is of value to their type of buyers.

- **Quality is their watchword.** It's not just any old content they share, just to please the search engines, but genuinely useful, well-produced, creative content that sets them apart from the crowd.

All of these companies put valuable content at the heart of their marketing. They turn their knowledge, expertise and ideas into information that is useful and meaningful to their types of customer. It is this information that they publish, promote and widely share. Potential customers get information that they can use, whether or not they buy from that company; the company builds goodwill and the result is more interest, more leads and more sales. Win:win.

It shouldn't need saying but it is worth pointing out – all these companies are *actively* marketing their firms. They are communicating consistently, taking action, doing stuff. Marketing has become part of their day-to-day activities, not an ad hoc campaign undertaken once or twice a year when leads run dry.

So these companies have learned to stop pushing so hard and start helping. Follow their lead and get online, really get to know your customers and commit to continually creating and sharing great content just for them.

Valuable Tip

Put your marketing focus firmly onto your customers and clients, and how you help them.

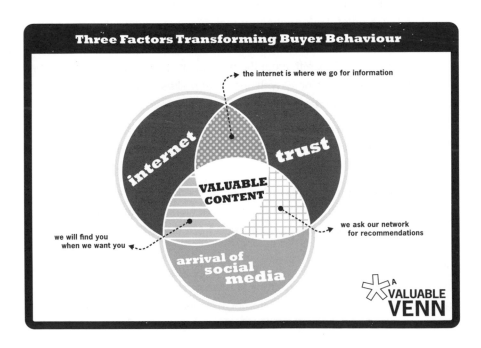

The three factors transforming buyer behaviour

Beating people over the head with your needs and desires to sell products and services isn't a successful strategy any longer.

Chris Brogan, Human Business Works **www.chrisbrogan.com** @chrisbrogan

Why is the valuable content approach so pertinent today and why are strong-arm marketing techniques heavy on self-promotion losing their impact? Let's take a closer look at three trends influencing the current buyer mentality.

1 The internet

2 Trust issues

3 The social web

The Internet has changed the game

Thanks to the Internet, marketing has evolved over the years. Consumers no longer rely on [sales people], billboards and TV spots to learn about new products, because the web has empowered them. It's given them alternative methods for finding, buying and researching brands and products.

Mashable **www.mashable.com** @mashable

In the past, if a potential customer wanted information on your type of services or product he would most likely call your company and engage one of your sales team to get the lowdown on your offer. He was more receptive to your direct sales and marketing campaigns because he couldn't get information on your company any other way.

Today his first port of call is undoubtedly the Internet. He'll search for answers using Google, ask his online social networks for recommendations and visit a few websites to assess his options. He is checking to see who he can best trust to solve his problem, and he now has access to all the information he needs at his fingertips to do just that. The Internet puts your customers and prospects firmly in control.

77% of all UK adults that use the Internet do so for finding information on goods and services. This is 80–85% for 35 to 64 year olds.

Office for National Statistics, Internet Access – Households and Individuals 2011

Whatever industry you are in the search is on. It is becoming increasingly obvious that the right content will get you found.

Companies that offer helpful content stand out

I was searching the other day for legal firms that specialized in helping schools convert into academies. It's a crowded market, yet one firm kept coming up top. This firm has created a straightforward and well-written guide that answered all my ground-level questions on the subject. It wasn't particularly visual; it simply laid out the key areas I needed to understand.

It won me over during this research phase. I didn't want to immediately 'ring for a free appraisal' – talking is something that comes a bit later, when you've orientated yourself in the area, and you know what you don't know, and where you need help.

This company had showed themselves to be authoritative, helpful and on the ball. They'll be the first place we go to when the time is right.

Governor – Hotwells Primary School

Valuable Tip

A web presence is absolutely essential to any business. If you want success in your marketing get online and provide the type of information your customers are searching for.

As the web becomes a more dominant force in helping businesses to grow and attract customers, the idea of putting valuable content at the heart of your marketing becomes more important. Valuable content is what allows you to be found in a sea of noisy competitors and to build a relationship with customers that you'll profit from.

It's not just the accessibility of information via the Internet that has changed buyer behaviour. It's the sophistication and proliferation of the web tools available to us. New and better tools mean we can create and publish content ourselves – with blogs, easy content management systems for websites, sites such as YouTube, Vimeo, Slideshare and social networks. We no longer have to pay for web developers to update our content or beg the paid media to publish our articles. We can wrest back control and do it ourselves, publishing our ideas and sharing our knowledge for free. This has opened up a huge opportunity for any business.

The dominance, accessibility and popularity of the web is only one of three major shifts that have collided to create the perfect storm and erode any effectiveness that less helpful, more self-oriented marketing techniques ever had.

We are selling and marketing to a world with little trust

Trust is at an all-time low. Trust in governments, trust in corporations, trust in salespeople, trust in marketing messages – all are lower than a grasshopper's knee. This is precisely what happens when organizations and their messages become self-serving – a focus that leads them to twist the truth in their favor, even to lie. As a result, they are not to be trusted.

Charles H Green, author of *The Trusted Advisor* **www.trustedadvisor.com** @charleshgreen

We live in an increasingly cynical world. The Edelman 2012 Barometer of Trust report presented at the World Economic Forum in Davos found that trust in governments reduced by 9 per cent in the last year to 43 per cent, and trust in business fell from 55 per cent to 53 per cent. Why does the crisis in trust affect your business? Why should we care? David Tovey, author of *Principled Selling* tells it like it is:

For those of us who have to sell a service or a product there was already plenty of suspicion that people who 'sell' things might just say or do anything to get a sale. It's a view held by too many people who sell; and worse, it's a view held by people who buy – even when the seller has the best of intentions. Today, salespeople (or anyone who looks like, sounds like or smells like a salesperson) risk not being trusted.

David Tovey, author of *Principled Selling* **www.principledselling.org** @principledsell

With this growing lack of trust and in the face of a deluge of self-serving sales messages we've learned to block out most of the noise: we ignore most promotional advertising; chuck blanket direct mail in the recycling bin; slam the phone down on cold callers; turn away in the face of 'spin'. We have been oversold to and we've had enough!

Who do we trust in a cynical world? Those who clearly have our best interests at heart: those who understand our situation, and try to help us – genuine, sincere people, not faceless corporations, those who give us information that is relevant and of value.

> The more you focus on others the more you will be trusted.

Charles H Green, author of *The Trusted Advisor* **www.trustedadvisor.com**
@charleshgreen

If you want success with your marketing, turn your back on self-promotion. Instead of saying how great you are, prove your expertise and your usefulness, your authenticity and your humanity. Build trust by helping your prospects and customers.

Valuable Tip

In a cynical world attraction, not promotion, is the key. Invest in providing valuable content.

The rise of the social web

> The good news is that there are now so many ways to demonstrate trustworthiness before ever trying to win business. It has never been easier to deliver valuable content via websites, blogs and social media to build credibility and trust.

Richard Wylie, Director of Questas Consulting **www.questas.co.uk**
@richard_questas

In recent years we have witnessed the meteoric rise of social media – it started with sites such as Friends Reunited then there was Facebook, LinkedIn, Twitter, YouTube, and now Google+, plus myriad other options and more on the way. Social networking using these new media has transformed our ability to communicate and connect online. In the UK 57 per cent of adult Internet users use the Internet for social networking according to the Office for National Statistics. You can no longer separate your company's message from 'technology' and social media.

According to the Edelman 2012 Barometer of Trust report:

- Against a backdrop of increasing scepticism around the world, trust in social media rose by 75 per cent in the year.

- Online search engines are now one of the most trusted sources of information for people searching for general news and information, new product information, etc.

- Among 18- to 29-year-olds, digital media is the most popular source for general news and information.

Impulse purchases aside, when we're looking to buy something, we ask around for recommendations before we do anything else. Whether it's a holiday or someone to help with our web design, the first thing we are likely to do is to ask the people we know. It is the referral nature of social media that makes it such a huge opportunity for your business. Social media has made it easy to build and communicate with a very large network, dramatically increasing the numbers of people we 'know' and who know us. Social media makes referrals very easy. It takes seconds to Tweet '*Who do you use to help with your accounts?*' The vast majority of your clients and customers will have trusted networks of friends and contacts they respect for advice and referrals, and now these networks can be accessed instantly online.

As we show in Chapter 5, social media is powered by great content. Share, Like, Tweet – posting and swapping links to valuable content is the oil that fuels the social web.

Valuable Tip

Social media is important if you want to get best results from the Internet – join the conversation.

The new buyer mentality

Thanks to the Internet we have access to information like never before and we'll make up our own minds: we'll find you when we want you. We don't want to be sold to.

Cold calling, sending out brochures, investing in costly press advertisements – these used to be the only weapons in the sales team's armoury, and they worked, some of the time. Things are different now. Strong-arm techniques hit the wrong note these days.

> *Uh oh, sales guy has just emailed with the words 'discount available if you sign up before the end of the month' – red rag to a bull.*
>
> Matthew Curry, Head of E Commerce, Lovehoney **www.lovehoney.co.uk** @lovehoney

Your audience won't accept the old-style hard sell. Cynicism is epidemic.

> *Really annoyed now – tempted to stop the whole sales process. I hate people trying to use sales tactics on me.*
>
> Matthew Curry, Head of E Commerce, Lovehoney **www.lovehoney.co.uk** @lovehoney

Just provide us with good information and we'll do what makes best sense to us, that's the new buyer reality. Don't try to manipulate us into buying. Focus instead on improving our lot.

Buyers prefer valuable content

> *Top three reasons why people go online? To learn stuff, to be entertained, to socialize: not to be sold to.*

Valuable content – whether it is educational, meaningful or just plain fun is the type of information that buyers seek and appreciate when they find it. Public opinion researchers 'Roper Poll' conducted research this year that backs this up:

- 80 per cent of business decision-makers prefer to get company information in a series of articles rather than an advertisement.

- 77 per cent of people understand that the purpose of an organization's content is to sell them something, but are OK with it as long as it provides value.

- 61 per cent say valuable content makes them feel closer to the company that delivers it and are more likely to buy from that company.

This is a real opportunity to get ahead of the game. These are really exciting times for those who align their sales and marketing approach with the new expectations of customers and clients. In a world with little trust, where information is at our fingertips, where Google is the place we turn to for answers, where social networks are trusted more than traditional media, valuable content is what we seek.

We get bombarded with dull, uninspiring sales messages all day and see them as an intrusion, rather than something of value. Of course, for that tiny minority of small businesses who DO produce marketing, which people genuinely value and would miss if it were to stop, the sky is the limit!

Jim Connolly, Jim's Marketing Blog **jimsmarketingblog.com** @jimconnolly

Valuable Tip

Educate or entertain your buyers, show them best practice, tell them what to look out for, give them valuable tips on how to achieve success, demonstrate how you've helped others in their shoes. Answer their questions and solve their problems, open their eyes.

Creating and distributing this kind of relevant, valuable and compelling information will help you turn prospects into buyers and buyers into long-term fans.

Take action

- What business development activities annoy you and which do you appreciate? Make a list.

- Think about the last time you decided to buy a product or service. How did you research, find and select your chosen product or service?

- Ask your current clients or customers – how did they find you?

Further reading

The Trusted Advisor, David Maisner and Charles H Green, Simon & Schuster, 2002

Trust-based Selling: Using customer focus and collaboration to build long-term relationships, Charles H Green, McGraw Hill, 2006

The Trusted Advisor Fieldbook: A comprehensive toolkit for leading with trust, Charles H Green and Andrea P Howe, Wiley, 2012

Principled Selling: How to win more business without selling your soul, David Tovey, Kogan Page, 2012

Inbound Marketing: Get found using google, social media and blogs, Brian Halligan, and Dharmesh Shah, Wiley, 2010

CHAPTER 2
WHAT IS VALUABLE CONTENT AND WHY IT WINS YOU BUSINESS

*You can **buy** attention (advertising)*

*You can **beg** for attention from the media (traditional PR)*

*You can **bug** people one at a time to get attention (traditional sales)*

*Or you can **earn** attention by creating something interesting and valuable and then publishing it online.*

David Meerman Scott, author of *The New Rules of PR and Marketing* www.webinknow.com @dmscott

In this chapter:

- What we mean by valuable content.
- The rise of valuable content as a smart marketing choice.
- Five vital things every business needs, and valuable content delivers.
- The wider benefits to your business.
- How valuable content connects you with your customers.

Find out why valuable content is the smart marketing choice for businesses today and how it wins you business, with stories from companies large and small.

What we mean by valuable content

Let's be clear on what we are talking about here.

'Content' is the words on the page you are reading. It's the copy on your website, the blog you posted last night, the videos and images you share. When we're talking about content, we just mean words, knowledge and information.

Valuable content is supercharged content. It's content with a bigger purpose; useful information created for a particular audience; content that hits the mark. By valuable content we mean the words, knowledge and information you choose to shape and share for your clients and customers: content that educates, helps or inspires them. Content they appreciate.

> *To be valuable, content must have uniqueness at the client level, and it must be meaningful.*
>
> Charles H Green, author of *The Trusted Advisor* @charleshgreen

Before embarking on marketing your business with content, you need to understand what makes certain types of content valuable, and why some types just don't hit the mark. Here is a quick quality control guide to help you ensure the content you create works for your clients and customers and for your business too.

Valuable content is:

- Useful – it educates, informs or entertains.
- Focused – it is relevant and meaningful to its target audience.
- Clear and compelling – it tells a story that people understand and respond to.
- High quality – it is interesting, well produced, with substance.
- Genuine – it is written from the heart by people who care.

In any combination, these attributes form just the kind of content that gets read, shared and acted upon. Businesses that really win exhibit all these qualities across the variety of content they put out there.

Like beauty, the value of a piece of content is in the eye of the beholder. What's valuable to me isn't necessarily valuable to you. This is how Sonja sees it:

The content that is valuable to Sonja

It's Monday morning. I sit at my desk with a packed week ahead. I open up Outlook and face the usual deluge of emails. I delete about 30 of them straight off (starting with the spammy ones I don't know and didn't ask for), but there are a few emails I always look out for:

- The niche newsletter from Recourses for marketing services firms like mine, which consistently gives me good ideas on how to run my business better.

- My timely 'Monday Morning Wave' email from *Surfers Path* magazine, with a stunning surf photo and links to interesting articles and videos on their site.

- Swimtrek's monthly missive about wild swimming, with tips on swim technique, photos of gorgeous places to swim and upcoming events I can join.

- Copyblogger's superbly written articles on writing and marketing on the web.

I valued the content on these companies' websites enough to sign up for their email updates in the first place; and I read them, even look forward to them despite the pressures on my time.

Now, don't get me wrong, I'm fully aware that all these companies are trying to sell me something:

- *Surfers Path* wants me to keep buying their magazine (and I do).
- David Baker of Recourses has a few books he could sell me (I've bought most of them).
- Swimtrek wants to encourage me to take up one of their swimming holidays (I have and if this book makes money I will again!).
- And Copyblogger wants me to spread the word, and sign up for more of their services.

But the content these companies share on their websites, in their emails, across social media doesn't major on the hard sell. Their marketing all starts from the premise of delivering valuable information to me, their kind of customer. They understand their customers well enough to know exactly what type of information we appreciate, and they focus their marketing communications on generously sharing their knowledge. Their marketing majors on delivering high-quality educational, informative and entertaining content – the kind that customers like me really appreciate.

This is valuable content – content that is generously shared and willingly received. This book will show you how to create it for your clients and your business.

The rise of valuable content as a smart marketing choice

Valuable content is set to become the number one choice for smart marketers and business owners. The 2012 research report by The Content Marketing Institute found that use of valuable content tools such as articles, social media, blogs and e-newsletters are all on the rise. White papers have increased in take-up 19 per cent, blogs and videos by 27 per cent. According to the Custom Content Council, 68 per cent of Chief Marketing Officers say they are shifting budget from traditional advertising to this type of marketing.

From micro-businesses to the giants such as Coca-Cola, valuable content is gaining traction.

Coca-Cola shifts from advertising to content

Coca-Cola has been wedded to traditional media and agency-led advertising since its inception over 100 years ago. In 2012 they announced in a series of beautifully produced YouTube videos that to hit their growth targets they are shifting their marketing attentions to sharing compelling content across social networks and the web in order to grow their businesses. Their marketing mission statement for 2012 onwards is 'Content 2020'. To win today, Coca-Cola recognizes that it must move from creative excellence to content excellence.

> *All advertisers need a lot more content so that they can keep the engagement with consumers fresh and relevant, because of the 24/7 connectivity. If you're going to be successful around the world, you have to have fat and fertile ideas at the core.*

Jonathan Mildenhall – Coca-Cola's VP of Global Advertising Strategy and Creative Excellence

Current take-up of a valuable content marketing approach differs across industries. In most reports we found that professional services led the way for this type of marketing (the latest CMI B2B Content Marketing Trends Report put this at 94 per cent adoption) closely followed by computing/software and marketing businesses. Confidence in valuable content as a strategic marketing tool is rising and businesses and marketers are devoting more and more budget to this approach. On average, 60 per cent of respondents indicate that they plan to increase their content marketing budgets over the next 12 months.

Marketing with valuable content is gaining wide acceptance as the way to get your message across today.

Hang on a minute. Is this form of marketing new?

The terms 'content' and 'content marketing' are relatively recent additions to the language of business, but the notion of giving a bit of valuable knowledge away for free in return for attention is nothing new. Michelin Guides, Jello recipe books, Lego magazines, and white papers from professional firms were generating interest and sales long before the Internet, but the web has given this approach wings. With the advancements in web technology and the arrival of social media it has become far easier and cheaper to publish and spread our ideas.

Good marketing has always been valuable but the difference today is that buyers no longer tolerate or respond to marketing that is less than good. Marketing the valuable way is an approach that's come of age; one that is starting to explode in popularity in all sectors of business around the world because of the results it brings. We want to show you how to make the most of this opportunity.

Five vital things every business needs, and valuable content delivers

The market has changed, and businesses need to find different ways of reaching out to clients and customers. If your business is to succeed in our Internet-dominated, low-trust social media age this is what you need:

1 a spotlight – so you get found;

2 star quality – so you stand out from the crowd;

3 buzz – so people talk about you and refer you;

4 shelf life – so they remember you when the time comes to buy;

5 personality – so they learn to like and trust you.

Valuable content delivers all of these things. Let's have a look at each one in more detail, with stories from companies who have put valuable content at the centre of their marketing and are getting great results.

A spotlight

You want your business to be found in a direct search by a buyer searching on the web: eg *'I want to find someone to help me with information security – information risk management advisers Ascentor came out on top in a Google search.'* And you want to be the company that gets stumbled upon in a general web search: eg *'I was looking for ideas on how to transform my IT department when I stumbled upon a very informative slideshow from management consultancy Formicio on the subject.'* Marketing your business with valuable content gives you a very strong web presence and gets you found.

Without valuable content on your website it might feel like you are whispering in the wind. This is the stuff that makes you findable and connects with potential clients when you get found.

Lee Duncan, author of Double Your Business @lee_duncan

Inksters get found through their content

Forward-thinking Scottish law firm Inksters Solicitors attracts new clients from the web. They have turned their website into a valuable resource for people looking for their services, putting their years of legal knowledge online. Their marketing focuses on creating and sharing valuable content in each of their niche areas and it's an approach that is getting them found.

One of their specialities is crofting law. Go to their website and you'll see pages of useful information, articles, videos, case studies, even lectures given on the subject. Search engines love all this content and reward Inksters with high page rankings, so if someone with a legal issue types in 'crofting law' Inksters website appears right at the top. People love it too. Their valuable content encourages people to think that Inksters is the right firm to do business with. The depth of information they provide proves their expertise and their utility.

Even in a traditional profession such as law, valuable content works. It gets Inksters found on the web, turns visitors into new clients (20 per cent of new business came from direct web search last year) and motivates even more referrals too.

See **www.inksters.com**

Valuable Tip

'If you don't tell the world about your professional expertise and achievements it is likely that only your existing clients and people they refer to you will know about them. Cast your net wider by publishing your knowledge, expertise and achievements online – you never know who might be searching for the specific assistance that you can provide', says Brian Inkster, Inksters Solicitors, **www.inksters.com** @inksters

uality

...are up against a competitor, valuable content gives you the edge; ...ives you lots of edges. '*It was clear they were more expert, more helpful, I could see what they were all about, how passionate they were about their subject. They looked like they were the kind of company we could work with. This gave them credibility and made me trust them.*' It's a way of demonstrating your expertise and value in a way that catches the eye. People gravitate towards businesses that make their content marketing valuable.

Newfangled stands head and shoulders above the rest

Web development is an overcrowded marketplace but Newfangled most certainly set their business apart. The quality and focus of their content gives them stellar status in their field. They differentiate themselves by focusing on a niche market (website development for advertising agencies and marketing firms).

Unlike many design firms their website is far more than a flat, online brochure. Their home page leads with valuable tips and articles for their audience, not flashy graphics or just an online portfolio. Their active blog, superb monthly newsletters, Twitter feeds, webinars and books help them attract, inform and engage the right audience. All this valuable content guides and educates their clients and wins them more work. It's turned their website into a lead-generating machine. President of Newfangled, Mark O'Brien explains:

> *Our content-rich website is the cradle of our marketing universe. It differentiates us and validates our expertise. The website is independently responsible for 20 per cent of our new business but its benefit to us is wider still.*
>
> *Because it does such a thorough job of documenting and sharing our expertise on a continual basis, it attracts the attention of many prospects, but also other key influencers in our field whom we are then able to foster relationships with. These relationships open doors which enable us to start engaging in a wide array of off-site marketing activities such as speaking at key industry events, publishing in industry journals, and publishing books through the right industry publishers.*
>
> *Valuable content is the foundation for all our marketing efforts.*

See **www.newfangled.com**

Valuable Tip

'When considering creating on-site web content for your customers, be sure to know what sort of client you're trying to attract, know what they are struggling with, and why they might hire you. Once you've figured that out, share your expertise generously,' says Mark O'Brien, President, Newfangled, Author of *A Website That Works* **www.newfangled.com** @newfangledmark

Buzz

Referrals are gold dust. Valuable content is an easy referral tool, and it gives people something to talk about and share. People are far happier to pass on something useful or compelling they've read or seen (it makes them look and feel good), than hand over the spare business card you gave them (in fact, they've probably lost that already). Valuable content builds your reputation and will prove the rightness of their referral.

Balsamiq grows on the strength of their referrals

Balsamiq is a software company with a simple and hugely popular website mock-up tool used by designers all over the world. From day one founder Giacomo 'Peldi' Guilizzoni blogged openly about his experiences, even giving away details of his revenue figures from the start. Written from the heart his blog quickly built an active community of followers who cheered him on and spread the word. All this goodwill and exposure helped his software go from zero to leader in just 18 months.

Today at Balsamiq everyone blogs. Peldi encourages each member of his team to become a leader of their chosen niche and share valuable content with their community. The Balsamiq website is rich with useful, authentic, inspiring content that helps their reputation grow and spread. Type Balsamiq into Google or search on Twitter and the buzz is clear for all to see. The results are remarkable: started as a one-man operation in 2008, by 2011 Balsamiq had cleared $5 million.

See **www.balsamiq.com**

Shelf life

Be remembered and easily found when the time comes to buy. '*Their articles were useful so I signed up to their mailing list, and they continued to send me relevant stuff. Now the time has come and I'm ready to buy they are the first people I thought about.*' Being in the right place at the right time is useful, and valuable content lets you do that. We will show you how to keep your business on that radar in a way your clients like.

Swimtrek are never forgotten

Swimtrek, a business selling wild-swimming holidays in the world's most stunning open-water locations, knows how important it is to keep in touch. Their monthly email newsletter is filled with content that is useful and inspirational for the wild-swimming community. They give away training and coaching tips to help people swim better, the kind of things a swimming coach would say during a private coaching session. Learn something simple that makes a fun activity even more enjoyable, and people want to share it.

Swimtrek customers spread the word in the pool, strike up conversations, help each other out. Its useful newsletter makes advocates of its customers. Throw in some inspirational stories of swimming in beautiful locations (Greek Island hopping without the ferry anyone?) and they've got people hooked. Swimtrek's marketing team doesn't need to invest in much other than the creativity required to produce a genuinely valuable content, with relevant, useful, inspiring information that really hits the spot.

See **www.swimtrek.co.uk**

Personality

Winning the marketing game means getting people to know, like and trust you and remember your business when the time comes to buy. You'll achieve this by sharing information that is important to your audience rather than being overly self-promotional. Valuable content gives you something to talk about that matters and a reason to engage. It shows your human side.

Intel shows its human side

Intel's processors are 'ingredient products': things that consumers cannot touch or feel directly. The company's marketing challenge is engagement – how do you give processor chips personality? By producing and sharing valuable content with the different communities that use the products – that's what Intel do.

Valuable content makes the brand real to people and helps them to engage. It's the centre point of their communications and the focus of their marketing today. Every day they create, curate and share content that informs, entertains, interests and engages. Visit Intel's 'Inside Scoop' website and you'll find a variety of blogs for different communities, useful tech tips, lively social media feeds and the processor art gallery.

Valuable content connects Intel with their market and makes them more likeable. It successfully gives a big technical corporate a very human face.

See **scoop.intel.com**

Valuable Tip

Think about how to make your business and your products more human and accessible to your clients. Getting your experts to blog in everyday language is one way, being creative and injecting personality through imaginative content projects that take inspiration from your products is another route.

The wider benefits to your business

As you can hear from the companies above, valuable content gets great results. It will: Position your company as interested experts; encourage people to ask you for advice; generate new and warmer sales leads; help existing leads move towards a sale; build your networks on social media; motivate more referrals; give your sales people a good reason to engage; help you be remembered when the time comes to buy; boost your search engine performance.

Content is one of your most cost-effective marketing investments. It just keeps on paying back. Post something useful online and it is there forever, generating interest for your firm.

> *Posts on my blog that I posted more than three years ago are still generating me hot leads today. What's more, if you're smart about using it, and re-using it, one piece of content can be used in various contexts – from a talk to many from a conference platform to a one-to-one sales chat over coffee.*
>
> Bryony Thomas, author of Watertight Marketing **www.bryonythomas.co.uk** @bryonythomas

Valuable content is the gift that keeps on giving. Do it well and you will transform your business development capability, and experience wider benefits too, as Top Consultant's story shows.

Top Consultant and a tale of two job boards

Top Consultant is a specialist careers website offering jobs in management consulting and Internet consulting. Since its inception in 2000 the company has built its business by sharing valuable content that people in the consulting sector and consultancy recruitment industry would find compelling.

They have become a hub of industry news, thought leadership and research, producing popular up-to-the-minute reports such as the annual 'Salary Benchmarking Report' – a comprehensive study of remuneration levels within the consulting sector.

All this content is free on their website and distributed via their monthly newsletter and active social media feeds. It is just what their audience wants, helping to generate around 125,000 monthly unique visitors to their site – 100,000 of whom are subscribed to their e-newsletters.

Top Consultant's business development model brings in the sales they need but it has wider business benefit too.

Top Consultant's business development model:

- **Focus on: Sharing valuable content motivates inbound leads**
- No need for outbound sales team
- No expensive commission structure

- Low turnover of staff
- Business is resilient to anyone leaving
- Excellent client retention

Contrast this with business development at another niche job board:

- **Focus on: Outbound sales to drive advertising take-up**
- 30–40 telesales people
- Large commissions to motivate performance
- High turnover of staff
- Drop in business when a good salesperson leaves
- Poor client retention

A focus on leading with valuable content has made all the difference to Top Consultant. It makes for a healthier, happier business.

See **www.top_consultant.com**

Valuable Tip

'Deliver content that is either unique, more engaging, more timely or more conveniently delivered than your competition. Businesses that get success from their content do at least one of these things really well.'

Tony Restell, MD of Top Consultant **www.top-consultant.com** @tonyrestell

How valuable content connects you with your customers

This kind of marketing really connects your with your customers. Let us explain with an example of the steps from content to customer for a professional firm today.

From web search to sale and beyond with valuable content:

1 A prospective customer has a challenge they want to solve.

2 They go onto the web and Google a specific search phrase.

3 They land on an article or e-book or video you've created on that very subject.

4 They read and learn from your content and are impressed with your insight.

5 They surf your website and notice that you specialize in the exact niche that concerns them most.

6 They take action, signing up for your newsletter or subscribing to your blog. They'll probably connect with you via social media too.

7 Over the next few months, they follow your blog or social media feeds and read your newsletter. Perhaps they also hear you speak at a conference. The more they hear from you, the more trust and respect they have for your professional insights.

8 They remember you and contact you when a need arises.

9 They refer you to their contacts too.

The second section of this book will show you how to create all the separate components in this cycle – the articles, blogs, e-books, videos, newsletters – and it will tell you how to join them up and distribute them, via social media and with a clear understanding of search engines too. Before we get on to the detail of the different tools, we need to share with you the golden rules for valuable content.

Take action

- Research the customer or client you'd love to win. What questions do they have?
- Map out the journey your buyers go through to become your customers.
- Note down what types of content you could create to answer their questions at each stage.

Further reading

Watertight Marketing: Delivering long term sales results, Bryony Thomas, Ecademy, 2013

Spiraling Up: How to create a high growth, high value professional services firm, Lee W Frederiksen and Aaron E Taylor, Hinge Research Institute, 2010

Duct Tape Marketing: The world's most practical small business marketing guide, John Jantsch, Thomas Nelson Publishers, 2006

Get Content, Get Customers, Joe Pulizzi and Newt Barrett, McGraw Hill, 2009

CHAPTER 3
'WHAT DO I SAY?' GUIDING PRINCIPLES FOR YOUR VALUABLE CONTENT

Walk a mile in your customer's shoes to help you decide on what sort of content they would find valuable. Don't just make it up. Ask them. What information would they appreciate?

Heather Townsend, Author of *The Financial Times Guide To Business Networking* www.joinedupnetworking.com @heathertowns

In this chapter:

- Seven guiding principles for your content (and a very different marketing mindset).
- How to find stuff to write about.
- Quick ideas starters.

In the first two chapters we examined why valuable content should be at the heart of your marketing efforts today. Like so many things, the world in which your business operates is changing, and new methods are coming to the fore. Before trying any new tactic it is useful to establish some solid foundations.

In this chapter we look at the attributes that underpin every piece of truly valuable content. We'll show you what these mean for your business and what you can do to prepare the ground for success with this marketing approach.

Hold onto your hats! This is not marketing as you think you know it. It is a different approach from most of the marketing you see (and ignore) today. Adopt a valuable marketing mindset.

Seven guiding principles for your content (and a very different marketing mindset)

Unthink what you think you know about sales and marketing communication. The valuable attitude is not 'look how great we are' (as in a traditional brochure) but 'see how useful we are – we have the answers to your problems'. Here are seven guiding principles to hold in your mind as you embark on creating valuable content.

1 Put your customers first.

2 Help, don't sell.

3 Give your knowledge away, for free.

4 Think niche.

5 Tell a good story.

6 Commit to quality.

7 Write from the heart.

Put your customers first

Don't be egotistical. Nobody cares about your products and services (except you). What people care about are themselves and solving their problems.

David Meerman Scott, author of *The New Rules of Marketing and PR*
www.webinknow.com @dmscott

As proud as you may be of your company/product/service, you should know that your customers or clients are not as interested as you are. Their only concern is how well you can help them to meet *their* challenges and needs. If you want more of them to buy from you, your focus needs to be on them, not on you.

Obsessive self-orientation is a mistake that many businesses make with their marketing communications. They are convinced that the purpose of their marketing is to continuously talk about how fantastic their company is; that the louder they shout, the better 'image' they put across and the more sales they will get.

Yes, of course the purpose of marketing is to help you to win more business, but if you want your marketing to be welcomed rather than seen as an irritation then shift your focus. Make every marketing communication primarily of benefit to the people who receive it and secondarily of benefit to you and your business. It's not rocket science; it's a simple awareness of human nature. And it will make all the difference to your marketing.

Practice management consultant Mel Lester demonstrates this customer-focused attitude perfectly. His desire is to create content that serves his clients and he leads his website with a strong promise:

> *Mel Lester is pleased to offer this website as a valuable source of 'how-to-get-things-done' information and tools. I set out with an ambitious goal: to create the best Internet resource for helping managers of architectural, engineering, and environmental consulting firms succeed, both corporately and personally.*

Taken from the home page of **www.thebizedge.biz** @mellester

Mel's statement demonstrates all the valuable attributes to aspire to. His content is helpful and focused, his goal clear and compelling. He has committed to content excellence and is evidently sincere in his desire to help. He focuses on the customer first.

If you are going to succeed with your marketing put your customer and client and their needs first, like Mel.

Quick test: How self-oriented is your website?

Take a look at your business websites or marketing material and try this test. How much of the wording is devoted to promoting the company? How much focuses on your potential clients and customers?

If you want to test your website's customer focus, try this simple online calculator – the 'We, We Test' from US marketers Future Now Inc.

Go to: http://www.futurenowinc.com/wewe.htm

This is a great tool for testing self-orientation and a great example of some seriously valuable content in its own right.

> **Valuable Tip**
>
> To make your content valuable, talk more about your clients and customers and their needs than you do about yourself and your business.

Help, don't sell

Focusing on your customers' needs rather than pushing your sales message? This can seem frustrating, like sitting on your hands. Although overcoming the desire to sell in your marketing communications might feel unnatural it is the only way to connect with cynical customers in our super busy world.

The purpose of your marketing is to build relationships – to get people to know, like and trust you, and think of you when the time comes to buy. Once you've gained your audience's trust and they grow to see you as a helpful advisor, they will choose to take the next step in your sales cycle. Build relationships first with valuable content and you will earn the right to sell.

It's no different to any other relationship. How do you feel when you go to a party and get stuck with the person who keeps talking about themselves, and their marvellous career, and their fabulous children? A bit bored, we'd guess. And how do you feel when you meet someone at the party who is interested in you, who asks you questions, and is obviously listening to what you say? You're far less likely to slink off to the kitchen at the earliest opportunity if you're talking to someone who shows a genuine interest in you.

It takes discipline and focus *not* to 'sell' with your marketing communications. But if you can restrain yourself from doing so and focus on delivering value instead, a funny thing happens: you win more business!

> **Valuable Tip**
>
> Whether you are writing content for your blog, your newsletter or even a Tweet, think 'How can I help?' not 'How can I sell?'. Provide value at every contact.

Give your knowledge away, for free

Think about it as 'commercial karma' – give your ideas, tips and advice freely and without expectation, it will come back to you in terms of referrals and reputation that will more than pay for itself.

Bryony Thomas, author of *Watertight Marketing* **www.bryonythomas.com**
@bryonythomas

The valuable content marketing approach means producing content that provides independent value to those who receive it, whether or not they choose to buy from you. This means giving away some of your hard-earned knowledge for free.

This simple principle throws up a lot of questions. Really, give my hard-earned knowledge away for free? Won't my competitors steal it and use it as their own? What is the right balance between sharing information openly and divulging a company's secret sauce? Here are our answers:

Q: Why should I give knowledge away for free?

A: Keeping your information locked up is not a great way to win business.

Deciding to buy takes a leap of faith. If you give away some value in advance people will start to trust that you know what you are talking about, that you are credible, reliable and helpful; that you are the kind of firm they'd like to work with and buy from.

You are not divulging secrets about your operations; you are giving away information that is of value to customers. The customers will see that you are the provider, and they will see you as the authority. This is what you want. Competitors will always be playing catch-up, but you will be setting the pace. Don't hide your expert knowledge for fear of losing it to business rivals – you'll miss an even bigger opportunity to connect with potential clients.

Q: Won't I lose my competitive advantage?

A: No, you'll gain more!

Back in the 1990s comedian Bob Monkhouse's joke book was stolen. Twenty-five years' worth of material lost. It didn't mean that whoever stole the book could win his work though. The missing material only had value when it was delivered by Bob Monkhouse. His timing, his delivery, his facial expressions turned the words on the page into comedy gold. And it's the same with your content. Giving away what you know won't mean other people can steal your business.

It's more than the information that makes people buy; it's the experience and the results we are after. That experience is unique to your business. No article or e-book is going to give away the sum total of the value you deliver to a client or customer. They won't be able to do it themselves. A few may try, but then they're probably not the type of client or customer you want anyway.

Q: How much should I give away?

A: You can afford to be generous.

In our view you can't give away too much. Put your best stuff online and share it. Think of it as 'commercial karma' – the more you give the more you'll get.

Here's the test: does it hurt a bit to give away this content? Good – that's the kind of content that will get you the best results.

Valuable Tip

'Give content freely, with generosity. If you're concerned about giving away too much or you're otherwise holding back in any way, worry less and give more.'

Andrea P Howe, President, BossaNova Consulting Group, co-author of *The Trusted Advisor Fieldbook* **www.andreaphowe.com** @andreaphowe

Think niche

The better we are at knowing our audience, the better we'll be at writing content they're likely to read and respond to.

Christopher Butler, Newfangled **www.newfangled.com** @chrbutler

The businesses that win in the digital age are the ones that have the greatest relevance to their target audience. They are the ones that are the most focused – they absolutely understand their market, their service and their customers.

To succeed with valuable content you'll need a laser focus on your customers or clients and their specialist needs. Take time to understand your market and their needs and position your content effectively. The way to get results is to specialize – stick your stake in the sand and target your content efforts at a particular niche.

> *Customers buy when they find that you are in their bull's eye – ie exactly what they are looking for. But the more bland and boring your marketing message, the more you become one of many in the outer rings of the target. When you have a niche – either by who you serve or by what you do – then you stand out as a specialist.*
>
> Paul Simister, Differentiate Your Business **www.differentiateyourbusiness.co.uk** @paulsimister

If you truly specialize you'll know more about your area of focus than most firms and you'll have something more relevant, unique and interesting to say. Your expertise becomes so much deeper.

For a larger firm serving many different markets this means creating specialist targeted content for each niche community you serve.

HSBC's niche site delivers value to the expat community

HSBC has recognized the need for targeted, relevant content. Take a look at their niche site for the expat community – www.expat.hsbc.com

With its specialist website, social media feeds, blog, YouTube channel, guides and tools, HSBC meets the specific needs of expat clients and customers and shows it understands them better than its competitors. @expatexplorer

See **www.expat.hsbc.com**

For a small firm with limited resources the niche question can mean some hard decisions – which market will you choose to serve? The subject of niche specialization is a contentious one for many smaller companies. The fear is that if you focus too narrowly you'll miss out on opportunities: seeking general appeal in large markets is seen as the safer option. But if you fail to specialize you run the risk of trying to be everything to everybody and failing to be remembered – your messages effectively disappear between the cracks. The more precisely you can describe your customers, address their issues and deepen your knowledge the more relevant and valuable your content will be and the more success you will get.

Having a niche makes your story so much easier to tell with your content, so much easier for people to understand and retell. Here is some sound advice from author of *The Art of the Start*, Guy Kawasaki:

> Put one niche in your basket, hatch it, put another niche in your basket, hatch it... and soon you'll have a whole bunch of niches that add up to market domination.
>
> Guy Kawasaki in *The Art of The Start* **www.guykawasaki.com** @guykawasaki

Action: Who are your dream clients and customers? What do they need? What issues and challenges do you solve for them? When should they pick up the phone to you?

Tell a good story

> Good content marketing is alive. It is your story. It is conscious. It is about emotion.
>
> Robert Rose and Joe Pulizzi in *Managing Content Marketing*

Good marketing has always been about telling great stories (think *Mad Men* and the age of advertising) and marketing in the digital age with valuable content is no different: good stories, great ideas – that's what gets spread.

Those who really get results unite their customers and content around a crusading central theme – a golden thread that runs through all the information they share. Being able to define your theme will unite your content and galvanize support for your ideas. Finding the mark where what you do intersects with what your customers truly want will give you a clear base from which to communicate.

Here are a few companies with a clear central message, an idea that spreads – they've got their positioning and their content just right:

- **Ascentor – Secure your information: strengthen your business.**
  In an industry that thrives on scaremongering, information risk

management consultancy Ascentor is a light in the storm. Their descriptive strapline focuses on the positive benefit they deliver for their customers. Their content all starts from this positive premise too. **www.ascentor.co.uk** @ascentor

- **The Red Cross – The greatest tragedy is indifference.** An emotional pull to take action if you care. **www.redcross.org** @redcross

- **Swimtrek – Ferries are for wimps.** This rallying strapline from wild-swimming holiday company Swimtrek is a big favourite for us. Committed wild swimmers smile and agree with its daredevil message, and this goodwill pulls them into the Swimtrek community. **www.swimtrek.com** @swimtrek

All these companies know what they stand for. Their various forms of content are anchored around a strong idea that connects with their customers and spreads.

Remember: valuable content is meaningful content. Don't just produce content; say something so good the reader forwards it on!

Commit to quality

'Make it fascinating', says Brian Clark of Copyblogger, 'entertaining, beautiful, fun'.

How do you create content so valuable it can't be ignored? If you really want to win, it has to be high quality. Aim for content excellence.

The content I regard as valuable is: useful and functional – gives me answers; beautiful and entertaining – gives me pleasure. It has to do at least one of those things. If it does both, I consider subscribing.

Jane Northcote, author of *Making Change Happen* **www.janenorthcote.com**

Content excellence relies on inspiration, creativity and also on good design. It's not enough to simply publish a very well-written article. The page that contains it needs to be styled to attract and focus the attention of the time-pressed reader. Your words need to be easy to read, on a webpage that is effortless to navigate, and a pleasure to look at. Whether it is written, video or audio, commit to quality. Great content needs great design and quality production to help it connect with its audience and make an impact.

> ## Valuable Tip
>
> 'How your content looks on the page is as important as the content itself. Take time to properly style your content. Use good quality photos and illustrations, clear text styling and design elements that compliment the look and feel of your website.'
>
> Justin Kerr, Creative Director of Newfangled Web Designers
> **www.newfangled.com** @newfangled_web

Write from the heart

Authentic, genuine, sincere – you can't fake value, although a lot of people try. It's a tricky line to follow; saying that you 'care about your customers' has become so much part of the corporate furniture we don't even notice it, let alone really believe it. Yet, to create valuable content you've got to care, and to want to make a difference to the lives of your customers. Having the right motivation behind the content you create will make a difference to how it is received. People can tell the difference between content that pays lip service to caring, and stuff that really means it. You will get more sales by being a good citizen with a genuine desire to help.

> *Sure, if you do a good job your company will benefit from the higher exposure and stuff... but that's a side-effect, not the end-goal. Becoming a leader in an online community is achieved by providing value to its members, continuously, over time. It means listening carefully and genuinely caring for the success of your fellow community members, without ever talking down to them – you're no better than them, you're just trying to help. It's hard work, but very fulfilling.*

Giacomo 'Peldi' Guilizzoni **www.balsamiq.com** @balsamiq

> ## Valuable Test
>
> Would you be embarrassed to send your content to a friend or someone who knows you really well because it is inauthentic?

If you want to create content that is valuable to your customers and clients and gets results for your business remember these seven principles.

Very quick checklist for each piece of content you create:

- Does it talk about the customer more than it does you?
- Is it focused on solving a particular customer issue or challenge?
- Will your target customer community find it helpful?
- Does it connect with your business message?
- Is it well produced?

How to find stuff to write about

Knowing exactly what to write about can feel like a hurdle. How can you make sure you produce content that reflects the valuable principles and really hits the mark with your target audience? Here are ideas to get your content on target.

Listen. What kind of questions do clients ask you? This chapter was prompted like that. People are always asking us 'but what can I write about?', so we're confident this chapter of the book is going to find a readership of people who are thinking about their marketing, who may want help at some time, or who would be happy to refer us as people who know useful stuff about content.

Valuable Tip

Keep a notebook. Jot down the questions you're asked. Answer them with five bullet points. Each question will form the basis of a short blog post.

Research. What are the big questions in your market? A quick jaunt around the relevant LinkedIn groups, or the liveliest forum in your industry will show you the issues that are raising a stir. Look at upcoming conferences – what are the speaker topics?

Valuable Tip

Pick the topic that catches your eye. Draft a simple Q and A blog post that deals with the topic from the point of view of your customers. Don't worry about being a 'thought leader' (you don't have to give the lecture!). Write about the subject as if you were explaining its relevance to a favourite client. What would they want to know about it?

Interview. Uncover your inner journalist and interview your clients, experts from your team, or someone in your industry that you admire. Ask them the questions your clients would ask you.

Valuable Tip

Use the interview as a podcast on your website, or the edited transcript as the basis for a blog post. Or two.

Survey. 92 per cent of people believe everything they read in surveys. Okay, so we made that up, but there's nothing like some interesting data to grab headlines, and make an interesting read.

Valuable Tip

Try LinkedIn Surveys or Surveymonkey. There are plenty of web tools that will let you do this for free. Frame the questions in terms your target market cares about. Use what you find for a blog post, or as fuel for an email marketing campaign.

Repurpose. What content are you sitting on? Most companies, if they do a quick audit, will realize they're sitting on valuable nuggets of content gold such as presentations, research created for a different context, information you wrote for sales proposals, talks you have given – even printed guides lying around. With some intelligent reworking you can get these online and make them available to a wide audience. Uncover your hidden stash of valuable content. Make the most of what you've already got!

You will find more ideas in Chapter 12, and our 'Get to know your customers' template in the Resources section.

Quick ideas starters

- Ask your clients and prospects – there's nothing better than a direct, face-to-face chat.
- Listen in to the top commentators or bloggers in your field – they have their ear to the ground.
- Set up Google Alerts on key terms to find out what's being talked about on the web.
- Twitter Search tools (eg Twilert) are useful – see what's trending on Twitter for your subject.
- Which of your blog posts get the most comment? Write more on that subject.
- What questions do you get frequently asked by clients in sales meetings? Answer them with a blog.
- Guest blog. Ask a related expert to write on your blog, and return the favour next month.
- Share an infographic that explains your ideas visually from a different angle.

With these ideas in mind, read on to the next chapter and get ready to get your content flowing.

Take action

- Go and check your website content: does it embody the seven principles of valuable content?
- Think about the content that grabs your attention on the web and that you feel compelled to pass on. Jot down what it is that you like about it.
- Complete the 'Get to know your customers' template in the Resources section.

Further reading

Content Rules: How to create killer blogs, podcasts, videos, e-books, webinars (and more) that engage customers and ignite your business, Ann Handley and CC Chapman, Wiley, 2011

The Go-Giver: A little story about a powerful business idea, Bob Burg and John David Mann, Penguin Books, 2010

The Art of The Start, Guy Kawasaki, Portfolio, 2004

PART TWO
WHAT VALUABLE CONTENT?

Your Valuable Content Universe

your newsletter

going stellar!

LinkedIn

Google

VC
your valuable content
website and blog

your sales
people

Twitter

other WWWs

CHAPTER 4
START WITH A BLOG

Many lawyers are no doubt too busy being lawyers to have time to blog. However, if they made the time to do it they might be even busier lawyers. But if they don't want to grow their businesses then fair enough.

Brian Inkster, Inksters Solicitors on The Time Blawg
thetimeblawg.com

In this chapter:

- Some blogging basics.
- Why blog?
- How to create a successful business blog.
- How to write a valuable blog article.
- A simple template for your blog articles.
- Blogging Q and A.

If you are committed to creating and sharing valuable content then a blog is the perfect place to start. Your blog will become the hub of your valuable content marketing activity. It is your number one content creation tool; your library, your store and the centre of your valuable content universe; a cost effective and rewarding way to start creating information that your customers will appreciate.

Writing and sharing articles has always been a powerful way to lay your claim to your territory, to show what you know, demonstrate your authority, and build up a following for your ideas and your business. In the past it was harder to do: you had to beg the paid media to publish your articles. With a blog every businessperson can now do this for themselves, for free.

The thinking that you do around creating a good blog will help you with all the other stages of your valuable content strategy. The only real cost is your time, and this chapter will show you how to use that time effectively for maximum blogging returns.

Some blogging basics

What is a blog?

The word blog is a blending of the phrase 'web log'. A blog is just a special type of website, a personal online publishing system that allows you to quickly and simply write, publish and distribute your opinions via the Internet on any subject you like. These appear in chronological order, giving the appearance of a journal-type format.

Blogs come in all shapes and sizes. For the purposes of generating business, what we mean by a valuable content blog is a place where you write about your subject for the benefit of the people you do business with – your personal spin on your area of expertise. A valuable blog is where you share your ideas in a form that is interesting and helpful to your customers.

What's not a blog?

A stream of promotional sales messages isn't a blog. A company news page isn't a blog either. 'We're happy to welcome Jane to the board', isn't really blog material, nor is 'We were thrilled to receive a mention in the local paper'. Yes, it's writing about your business, but blogs are helpful, they take a personal view, and demonstrate thought. Straight reporting of facts isn't a blog, nor is PR puffery.

Why blog?

Aside from the very real benefit of writing regularly about your area of expertise – in a way that your customers appreciate and find helpful and therefore stoking up a lovely warm feel-good factor around your business – blogs are a big hit with search engines. The more genuinely useful content your business blog contains around the terms your customers are searching for, the higher your rating will be and the more traffic you will get. The more you blog, the more you increase your reach to customers who stumble upon these blog articles while they're searching for answers to their problems and like what they find.

A blog demonstrates that you're a doer, as well as a thinker. You are working in the areas your clients are interested in, and have hands on, up-to-date experience. It's an easy way of showing, not telling, what you're up to – you're a busy professional who absolutely knows your stuff.

> *A blog will help people see past the commercial literature and engage with your business and your people.*
>
> Heather Townsend, author of *The FT Guide to Business Networking*
> @heathertowns

Seven reasons to blog

1 To spread the word about your business more widely and draw people to your site.
2 To give people a reason to keep returning to your website.
3 To build your reputation and lay claim to your territory.
4 To show your human, approachable side.
5 To help your clients and customers.
6 To improve your website's search engine ranking.
7 To get better at what you do.

To illustrate these points, here are three stories from valuable bloggers.

Jim's blogging story: confessions of a convert

Jim O'Connor is a copywriter who started a blog to go alongside his business website. He has been writing copy for about 20 years and only came across the concept of writing 'content' relatively recently. At first he wasn't keen on the whole idea – he felt it went against the grain of everything he believed about the craft of concise copywriting. Twelve months later with a successful blog, Jim's feelings are totally reversed. He now realizes that, when content is truly valuable and well presented, it's a really smart way for a business or individual to build their reputation.

> *As I began to experiment with creating and sharing valuable content on my blog it became apparent that it's not just valuable for the reader – it's also immensely valuable to the company providing it. Not just because it creates traffic and loyal readers who either spread the word or become customers (often it's both), but because it gives that company a way to share its knowledge and experience in a manner that just doesn't work in sales copy. They become a trusted go-to expert in their field and build long-term relationships with people they would otherwise never have been able to reach through traditional media. How valuable is that? It's priceless.*

> *So, I'm a convert. Writing content that has value for people is something I find immensely satisfying – not least because it's attracting a string of new clients who now appreciate just how I can help them. It's easy to be sceptical (I know, I was). But try it for a few months and you'll be amazed at the results.*

Sharing two or three articles a month on his blog gets people visiting and revisiting his website. Jim has picked up a number of regular contracts as a result, and his existing clients have started to use him for a wider variety of projects as they realize the full scope of his expertise.

See **www.storiesthatsell.co.uk/blog**

Ian Brodie swaps his traditional website for a blog

Ian Brodie is a business development consultant offering marketing and sales advice to professional firms. Ian swapped his traditional website for a blog-based one with remarkable results. Here is his story.

> *I decided to invest in a new website a few years ago. Like many business owners I was incredibly frustrated with my existing site. I'd stumped up quite a bit of cash for what I thought was a good-looking website. I had testimonials, case studies, service descriptions – everything. Well, everything except clients.*

> *Almost no one came to my site and those that did visit didn't hang around for long.*

> *I already had a separate blog – just for fun really: an outlet for my desire to share ideas on marketing and business development. I noticed that my pretty scruffy-looking blog far outstripped my professional website in terms of traffic, and in terms of the connections it allowed me to make with my potential clients and peers in my niche.*

> *Because my blog had useful content on it, other websites and blogs had no hesitation linking to it and highlighting my articles to their readers.*

Visitors stuck around far longer on my blog. They made comments. Some of them even emailed me to ask questions. I emailed back and we began to build a relationship. This never happened with my corporate site.

I started getting emails from people asking how I could help them in their business. Clients were coming to me!

In the end I abandoned my professional, corporate website. I got the blog tidied up and put all the stuff about my clients and my services as sub pages of the blog. I kept the focus of the new site firmly and squarely on delivering what you call 'valuable content' to keep readers engaged and coming back for more – and to get other sites linking to me to raise my Google rankings.

And the results? Thanks to this strategy I now get the majority of my clients via my website – and as I'd hoped, I don't have to go out and trade my time when I need new clients.

See **www.ianbrodie.com**

HSBC Expat Explorer – A great example of a valuable corporate blog

Corporate institutions like banks and blogging don't naturally go hand in hand, but HSBC has created a thriving blog site that reaches out to a section of its customers. Their Expat Explorer blog is a place for people to share their experiences of living abroad. Rome might look beautiful, but what's it really like living there? How easy is it to set up a bank account in China? What are the schools like in Bangkok?

Expat Explorer generates some excellent content of its own – the annual Explorer Survey turns up some fascinating, genuinely useful and beautifully presented findings, but what gives Expat Explorer its real strength is its generous sharing of content written by its audience. It links to blogs created all over the world, written in language a world away from corporate speak.

The HSBC Expat Explorer blog creates a genuine sense of community, and its lively Twitter feed encourages more engagement.

See **www.expatexplorer.blogspot.co.uk**

How to create a successful business blog

Great business blogs come in all shapes and varieties – from expert blogs to CEO blogs, from technical blogs to inspirational blogs. Each has a very different style and tone and different objectives to achieve. What defines them all is the passion of the people who write them. The best blogs are not necessarily written by those who know the most, but by people who care deeply about their subject and want to communicate with their audience.

You don't necessarily need thousands of followers and worldwide recognition to call your blog a success. However, it must be designed so that it constructively and efficiently helps your readers find the information they want and helps your business achieve its overall goals.

Tips for launching a successful blog:

- **Plan carefully.** Have a clear set of objectives for your blog.
- **Focus, focus, focus.** Don't try to be everything to everyone. Target your blogging efforts at a particular issue or a narrow niche and deliver.
- **Relevant and interesting content.** Understand what your audience needs and deliver a blog that is packed full of valuable content.
- **Good design.** Put some effort into design if you want your blog to be remembered and read. There are a lot of very good, free templates out there but if you want to stand apart invest in a good designer to make it yours. Use images in your posts to lift the text.
- **Vary the style.** Mix it up to keep the reader's interest. Get your message across in a variety of ways over time.
- **Promote your blog.** It's not 'build it and they will come'. Tell people the blog is there and keep telling them. Mention your blog on your various company and personal profiles, latest posts in your email sign off; share the articles on social media.
- **Launch it.** Get a few good starter posts in place and then launch it to your contacts. Invite them to sign up.

You will find links to blogs we rate highly in the Resources section at the end of the book.

How to write a valuable blog article

So, your business can benefit from a blog, and you've got some ideas for your first article. Sounds like you're ready to go! You need to give yourself some time – say two to three hours for your first article (you will get quicker) – and a bit of peace and quiet (shut the door, turn off distractions).

What to write about? Here are some ideas to get you started:

20 blog topics to inspire you:

1 Lists of tips or ideas, like this one. Numbered lists work well.

2 Reviews of books that you recommend.

3 'How to' articles.

4 Your comment on news that's relevant to your clients.

5 'Why?' articles.

6 Articles stating the benefits of your recommended approach.

7 Your response to a question you have been asked by a prospect or client.

8 Articles that state what your clients should avoid like the plague.

9 Add a seasonal twist – refer to a recent celebration or seasonal event.

10 An interview with one of your clients or customers.

11 A critique of someone else's article or opinion, with your view on what works or what does not.

12 Like a journalist, review what you learned from a recent talk, industry conference or event.

13 Ask other experts a question and share their response.

14 A case study on a company you have worked with or who can demonstrate success in your field

15 Conduct a survey and share the response.

16 A round-up of topical news for your community.

17 Share slides from a recent presentation you have given.

18 Feature guest posts/articles from experts in your field.

19 Information on products or services that will benefit your audience.

20 Share or create a cartoon or graphic that sums up your argument nicely.

Valuable Tip

Choose four suggestions from the list and start jotting down blog article ideas.

Over time you are aiming to build up a body of work that demonstrates a deeply layered understanding of your field and the way you can help navigate clients through it. Varying your blog approach and style adds value and will widen your reach – some people love quick 'how to' guides, others appreciate deeper analysis of key questions – but you have to start with one, so pick the one that sparked the most ideas, and that you feel most comfortable with, and begin.

A simple template for your blog articles

Here's a basic template to help you structure a valuable blog article:

Title. Headlines are hugely important. Tell readers what they'll learn by reading your article. Use the keyword in the title, and don't try to be too clever. Vague, intriguing titles can fall flat on blog articles; save your creativity for when you're promoting your blog online.

'Five incredibly simple ways to get more people to read your content' is a good blog title, but 'Make it snappy' doesn't work. Make it snappy could well be one of the points you make in the course of the article, but it's not strong enough as a title, even though it's very, err, snappy. Titles play an important role in search engine optimization, and your blog will add more to your online value if you tie it to the words your potential readers will be using to make their searches.

First sentence. You need a hook here. Ask a question; throw up something interesting or unusual. Grab attention. 'No one's reading a word you write' could be a good opener for the article, but 'Opinions are divided as to the best way for a writer to hold the attention of readers' wouldn't work; too long, too vague, not punchy enough.

Next paragraph. Get quickly to the point of your blog. Web readers skim rather than dig deeply, so no long preamble or sideways digressions. You've set out the question; start answering it straight away.

Bulleted list. Numbered or bulleted lists are great for blogs:

- They add structure.
- They allow you to pack in lots of valuable content without a lot of extra word padding.
- They feed web readers' hunger for answers *now*.

> **Valuable Tip**
>
> How many points on the list? Up to 10 works best. We are all busy. A shorter list reassures readers that this is going to be a quick win read, not *War and Peace*.

Image. Find a picture to illustrate your point: professional or quirky, stylish or funny, whatever fits your brand. You want readers to stick around, and a well-designed page with a strong visual appeal is more likely to keep them than a wall of unbroken text. (Stock photo sites on the web are a source of reasonably priced images.)

> **Valuable Tip**
>
> Be consistent when using images in blogs, keeping them the same size, for example, or in a similar style.

Question. You want people to engage with you through your blog, so encourage dialogue by asking a question at the end, throwing the floor open for comments. Blogs are unashamedly opinionated, so ask to share other people's views.

Respond. When people comment on your blog, make sure you respond. Build engagement through your blog, and it's more likely to get shared. And it goes without saying, you should respond generously, thanking people for taking the time to comment in a brief reply. If you have lots to say, you can always continue the conversation with the reader via email. (Obviously, you don't have to respond nicely to the spammers, or the obvious loons. It's your blog, do moderate it and feel free to trash comments that are way off the professional mark.)

Valuable Tip

An invaluable feature of any blog is the '**Share this**' button. A 'share this' button will make it really easy for people to pass on your content, if they like it. Without 'share this' they'll have to go back to Twitter or Facebook, or wherever they found the link, and do it from there. And they might get distracted, the phone could ring, something else will divert them away. 'Share this' is your chance to strike while the iron is hot, and make the most of the few seconds when your reader is still with you, and keen to tell other people about the brilliant thing they've just learnt.

If you liked this, try this. Another way of capitalizing on the enthusiasm your blog will have stirred is to guide the reader towards other blogs you've written on similar themes. Highlighting other relevant articles will pull them deeper into your website, showing them other ways that you can help. For example, if they'd found you via '10 things you need to know about e-commerce' they might well be interested in 'E-commerce platforms compared', or 'E-commerce case studies' or 'E-commerce snarl-ups and how to avoid them'. By offering your readers more layers of help, you're demonstrating an easy control over your subject matter, and a generosity that will make them well-disposed towards you. Embed the links to the other articles through the relevant catchy headlines, so that more help is just a click away.

Quick checklist for your blog articles:

- Will my target readers find this subject interesting and useful?
- Is the post in-line with our field of expertise/what we want to be known for?
- Does the headline have impact?

- Does it include keywords people would search for to find us?
- Does it have a clear beginning, middle and end?
- Can they read it over a cup of tea? (If it takes longer cut it back.)
- Have I stripped out any jargon?
- Have I broken up the text with useful subheadings and bulleted lists?
- Have I asked a question at the end?

You'll find a full blog template and structure to follow in the Resources section at the back of the book.

Blogging Q and A

Q: How often do I have to blog?

A: Just one blog a month will bring you benefit. Two a month is an ideal start for better results. Up the frequency as your confidence grows. One blog a week will make a huge difference to your business in terms of inbound leads.

> ### Valuable Tip
>
> 'Blogs need content, but you don't have to break your back creating it. In most niches, updating a blog with 1–3 highly valuable content pieces each month is enough', says Derek Halpern on the DIY Themes blog **diythemes.com/thesis**

Q: What do I write about?

A: See Chapter 3. People use the web to search for information, to research problems, or to be entertained, so you need to fit your blogs into one of those categories. Your best bet is to write articles that give the information people are looking for and provide the answers to their problems.

Q: I don't think I have anything to say.

A: This is a common fear. Look again at the list of 20 suggested topics. Write down the single most common question people ask you about your product or service. Then write down the answer you give them in 10 sentences. Voila – you have just created the draft of your first blog!

Valuable Tip

'Don't be afraid of not knowing enough. Remember, your bread and butter is somebody else's rocket science. Keep it simple and relevant to your audience', says James Chapman, Managing Director, Development Done Right **www.developmentdoneright.co.uk**

Q: Should the blog be part of my website or separate?

A: If it sits comfortably alongside your website, complementing the information there then integrate it or at least link the two very clearly. But if you are looking to present an objective view on your industry or think it needs a separate identity and brand then choose a different URL and run the blog independently.

Q: But I really hate writing, do I have to do it?

A: Read our writing tips in Chapter 13, use our blogging template and give it a go. It's a skill, like anything else, and you will quickly get better with practice. Think of your blog as a friendly conversation with a potential client, rather than a tough sales presentation in front of hundreds, and the words should flow more easily.

Valuable Tip

'I dislike writing so I developed a simple template for quickly writing a Q&A Column. The Question is 50 words, then my answer is made up of 4 parts, of 50 words each – Start, Middle, 3x Bullet Points and End. Total = 250 words, 1 hour', says Robert Watson, Managing Well **www.managingwell.com.au**

Q: Is there no other way? What about ghostwriters?

A: Of course, an alternative to blogging would be to find a freelance writer to help you. Find someone whose writing style you like, and who understands your industry. If you find talking much easier than writing, ask the writer to interview you and shape your words into a blog article that reads with your voice, but it's your ideas that should shine through. It's your business.

> ## Valuable Tip
>
> 'I write my articles by Dictaphone, so I can blog wherever the inspiration strikes.' Chris Budd, MD Ovation Finance **www.ovationfinance.co.uk** @ovationchris

Q: I'm way too busy, what can I do?

A: If you have a high level of expertise, and you want to build your business, then blogging is a very effective use of your time. Make time, and the effort will be repaid. No business can ignore online marketing, and your blog is the best way of showing potential clients what you can do.

Work it into your week – create a system and a time that works for you – see CFO Richard Edelman's *6am Blog* for example (**www.edelman.com/speak up/blog**). Richard, like many executive bloggers, fits it in by writing outside the 9–5 working day.

> ## Valuable Tip
>
> 'I write a lot of my blogs on the train. It's a great use of my time. I know the format inside out now, and I can usually get one done between Bristol Temple Meads and London Paddington.' Lizzie Everard, graphic designer **www.lizzieeverard.com** @lizzieeverard

- Consider getting freelance help from a writer.
- If dictating some blog ideas, and answers to customer questions, will fit more easily into your day, then start your blogging route with some external support.
- Share out the responsibility with the team. Make a plan and lighten the load.

Valuable Tip

'Look through your current list of clients, and drop the one who is your worst customer. This will initially free up time for you to write a blog. Then, as your valuable content marketing kicks in, you will have created some space for new and better clients!'

Robert Watson, Managing Well **www.managingwell.com.au**

Q: How short is too short?

A: Short and punchy is better than long and verbose. It's a good idea to aim for a high quantity of short (200–500 word) articles, rather than one 2,000 word one. Save the longer form content for a discussion paper or e-book.

Valuable Tip

Feed people's hunger for quick answers now by breaking down what you know into small chunks that can be easily digested.

Q: Can blogging damage my business?

A: Not if you do it well. It will build your business. Blogging is only damaging if you are:

- Inconsistent – saying one thing in one article and contradicting it in others.
- Lacking a clear direction – if your blogs are rambling, people won't be convinced of your authority.
- Jargon-filled/confusing – if people can't understand what you're saying, you won't feel like the right person to help them.
- Continually selling in your blog articles – this is not the place for overt sales messages.
- Slow to update your blog so it was last updated a long time ago.

Follow the valuable principles we talked about in Chapter 3.

Q: How do I set one up?

A: You have a variety of good options here. Look at Wordpress Blogger or Typepad, the top blog platforms. You'll find a host of free templates or some excellent paid themes with more sophisticated functionality and pre-set professional design. You can set one up yourself for free but for best effect commit to quality and invest in some design (blog header, and overall styling) to make the blog yours and set your business apart.

Take action

- Find three good blog posts. Print them out, then look at the way they're constructed – circle the headline, opener, main body, conclusion, and call to action.

- Write the blog post you choose from our list, using the template in the resources section.

- Show the blog to a colleague for feedback – getting used to sharing your words is part of becoming a good blogger.

Further reading

The Corporate Blogging Book, Debbie Weil, WordBiz.com, 2010

Subscribe to www.copyblogger.com for more blogging inspiration @copyblogger

CHAPTER 5
DISTRIBUTE YOUR VALUABLE CONTENT USING SOCIAL MEDIA

Social media didn't create content marketing, but it's an unsurpassed tool for getting it distributed.

Copyblogger www.copyblogger.com @copyblogger

In this chapter:

- Social networks – the main arenas for businesses.
- Which tool is best for sharing content?
- Valuable content guidelines for all social networks.
- Vary the content you share by platform.
- How to be valuable on Twitter.
- How to be valuable on LinkedIn.
- How to be valuable on Facebook.

Great content doesn't spread itself. Without help it can sit on your website or blog, untroubled by visitors, and not reach the desks and minds of the people it was written to engage. Something is needed to get your content from A to B, and that something is social media.

Your followers on your chosen social networks will see what you've written, and if they like it they'll share it with their contacts, who in turn might share it with theirs, and so on. Valuable content creates a ripple effect, spreading your ideas across your network and around the world.

This chapter will explain why you need to make social media part of your valuable content approach, and will give you the lowdown on the various social networking options open to you, and the best ways to navigate them for your business.

Social networks – the main arenas for businesses

Social networking sites such as Twitter and LinkedIn enable busy professionals to manage large networks of contacts – many times larger than is possible face-to-face. They generate consistent opportunities for those prepared to invest time in them.

Heather Townsend, The FT Guide to Business Networking,
joinedupnetworking.com @heathertowns

Which social networks will work best for your business? We are conscious that the landscape is changing fast. The tools we mention today will date, but one thing we're confident of is that embracing social media is crucial to the success of marketing your business with valuable content.

At the time of writing there are three main social networking channels for the business owner – Twitter, Facebook, LinkedIn.

Twitter

Twitter is a serious business tool. It builds important relationships and will help you market your business. It's an unrivalled marketplace for sharing your valuable content, building relationships and engaging with potential clients. Tweets are limited to 140 characters, so there's no room for waffle. Add links from your Tweets back to your blogs, and you will generate more traffic to your site. It's possible to build really powerful connections on Twitter, fantastic both as a way of attracting people to your content, and expanding your network and motivating referrals.

Should your business be on Twitter?
Yes! Any business in any sector will benefit from being on Twitter.

Valuable Tip

'Everyone loves a generous person sharing information freely. Share information on Twitter that your customers will value, and people will follow you.'

David Gilroy, MD of Conscious Solutions, **www.conscious.co.uk** @consciousol

Facebook

With 800 million users worldwide, Facebook has become the world's biggest meeting place and social networking site. You'll find big brands there, as well as pages for businesses. Facebook works by sharing your content with your friends, who in turn share it with theirs and so it spreads. 'Like' something on Facebook, and potentially it will be seen by thousands.

Fun, lively, crowded, Facebook is great for some businesses, not so good for others; chemical companies, heavy industry and construction firms, for example, would have a hard time making it work. Brands like Starbucks have embraced it, upmarket high street retailers like John Lewis are here, your customers and clients probably have personal accounts, setting up a page is free, and very easy.

Should my business be on Facebook?

It depends. Take the quiz below to find out.

Your Business	Yes/No
Are you in the travel, food, hospitality or leisure industry?	
Do you have lots of good pictures and video content to share?	
Does your business interest people beyond their working lives?	
Does your business inspire people?	

If the answer's 'yes' to all the above, then Facebook is for you.

Your Business	Yes/No
When you talk about your business at dinner parties do people's faces light up?	
Is your business a source of great anecdotes?	
Do you help your clients achieve personal ambitions, not just work goals?	
Does your business create loyal fans who love to share what you do?	

If the answer's 'no', then divert your energies elsewhere.

In essence if you are a B2C company then Facebook is likely to be a valuable place to be. If you are B2B then LinkedIn is more likely to get you the kind of attention, connections and exposure you need. There are exceptions of course... there always are.

Barry James, Social Media Architect, Fusion Revolutions, FusionRevolutions.com, @BarryEJames

LinkedIn

We've attracted over £40K of new business from LinkedIn alone in the last year.

David Gilroy, Business Development Director at legal web development firm Conscious Solutions

The professional networking site, LinkedIn is much less frivolous than Facebook, with space to say more than on Twitter. It's a business networking tool. Use the 'status update' feature to share your valuable content with your network. Commenting on other people's discussions, and starting your own threads is great for raising your profile, although the 'help, don't sell' mantra still holds. With over 100 million users worldwide, and highly ranked by Google, it will help you get found, make and maintain connections, build relationships and keep you front of mind.

Four important elements from a content perspective:

- Personal profiles – valuable for referrals.
- Status updates – to distribute your valuable content.
- Company pages – useful for building the credibility of your company.
- LinkedIn groups – worthwhile forums for connecting with others in your field.

Should I be on LinkedIn?

Yes! Every business professional should have a personal profile at the very least.

And the rest

There are many other social media options, all with significant followings. Here is a quick introduction to the best of the rest. You'll find further reading if you are interested in these at the end of the chapter.

Google+

Launched in 2011, this platform is growing in importance and popularity. Secure a presence here if you want to make the most of Google's enhanced search function. Social sharing is going to dominate search engine rankings over the coming years – Google will deliver search results based on what people are saying and recommending to each other, over and above simple keyword searches. It is a social network indexed by Google and, as Google is the number one search engine, it's useful to make a start here.

Google+ has longer form content than Twitter or LinkedIn – you have space to present and share more information in a variety of formats. We like the way it allows you to choose who you share information with, and it's very intuitive to use – easy to update, easy to upload pictures and videos.

Should I be on Google+?

At the moment, Google+ serves a B2B audience, so be here if you want to share thoughts, ideas and content and raise your personal profile.

> ## Valuable Tip
>
> The decision to use Google+ should be focused more on the ability to be found than the ability to win work. If your website is the hub of your activity, then Google+ should be seen as just another spoke in your armoury to earn attention for the company.
>
> Julian Summerhayes, Brand You, **www.juliansummerhayes.com**

YouTube

This is the world's biggest video sharing site and it's growing all the time. YouTube's head of global partnerships, Robert Kyncl, predicts that soon 90 per cent of all Internet traffic is going to be video, with YouTube being far and away the biggest channel. Setting up your own YouTube channel is an easy way to share your business video content with the world.

YouTube is not just a video content streaming site. It's also a social networking site, because of the way it allows you to connect with others and create a community. Set up a YouTube account and you can comment, rate, favourite and share videos that are relevant, interesting and helpful to your type of customers. All of this helps to send traffic back to your website. You don't even need to load up your own videos to do this, although evidently it will bolster your authority if you do. There are a lot of ways to use the platform to inform people, get them to participate, and grow awareness of your organization.

Here are YouTube's tips for making the most of this platform:

- **Reach Out.** Post videos that get YouTube viewers talking, and then stay in the conversation with comments and video responses.
- **Partner Up.** Find other organizations on YouTube who complement your mission, and work together to promote each other.
- **Keep It Fresh.** Put up new videos regularly and keep them short – ideally under five minutes.
- **Spread Your Message.** Share links and the embed code for your videos with supporters so they can help get the word out.

- **Be Genuine.** YouTube has a wide demographic, so high view counts come from content that's compelling, rather than what's 'hip'.

You'll find more on creating and sharing video in Chapter 10.

Pinterest

At the time of writing Pinterest is the newest of the Next Big Things on social media. The take-up it is getting is impressive. Launched in March 2010 the site registered more than 7 million unique visitors in December 2011, up from 1.6 million in September that year. And it's driving more traffic to company websites and blogs than YouTube, Google+ and LinkedIn combined, according to a report from US based content-sharing site Shareaholic.

Pinterest is an online bulletin board, where people share their favourite images, and comment on, share and 'like' other people's. Like Facebook, Pinterest has great potential for businesses that have visual content to share: retailers, travel companies, fashion businesses, anything to do with food and drink, home and gardening, photographers, wedding planners.

SlideShare

SlideShare is the world's largest community for sharing presentations. With 60 million monthly visitors and 130 million pageviews, it is amongst the most visited 200 websites in the world. Besides presentations, SlideShare also supports documents, PDFs, videos and webinars. Excellent for sharing your content, getting inspiration for new ways of looking at your material, and for helping your content find a wider audience.

Flickr

This is Yahoo's online photo sharing site. If your business creates lots of beautiful visual images, Flickr is a very good place to share them and engage with contacts.

Instagram

Instagram is a smartphone app that lets users add different filters to their own photographs, and share the images with the online community. Jamie Oliver (beautiful food photography, lots of engagement) and Red Bull (sharing photos of events worldwide with 10,000 followers) are early adopters of Instagram for brand building. Recently acquired by Facebook.

Which tool is best for sharing content?

The Content Marketing Institute's 2012 B2B Content Marketing report gives a helpful snapshot of the percentage of marketers using each platform to distribute content.

- Twitter 74 per cent;
- LinkedIn 71 per cent;
- Facebook 70 per cent;
- YouTube 56 per cent;
- SlideShare 20 per cent;
- Google + 13 per cent;
- Flickr 10 per cent.

Twitter, LinkedIn and Facebook are responsible for the most sharing. Which you choose to focus on depends on what type of business you are in and what is right for your customers.

In our experience, it has been Twitter that works best. We believe it's an unsurpassed tool for spreading valuable content around the web. Through Twitter we have connected with some fantastic people and won new work. It has helped us to build our business.

Valuable content guidelines for all social networks

The key in social media is to share things of value.

Charles H Green, Trusted Advisor

There are many different social media options and there will be others to come, but if you want to get the best results across any social media platform the same rules apply across all networks.

Here are seven valuable content guidelines to bear in mind, whichever network you select:

1 **Be there.** Join the conversation – be sociable, communicate – show up regularly.

2 **Be valuable.** Be helpful, entertaining, educate your clients – become a valuable source of information for others.

3 **Be generous.** Be generous in the content you share and generous to others too. Share other people's content. If it is valuable to your kind of customers then help them find it.

Chris Brogan, President of Human Business Works, and a social media expert advises you to make 10 Tweets about others for every one Tweet you make about yourself. Become known as someone who offers things up to others, and people will come to you.

4 **Be interesting.** Mix it up – all sorts of different types of content Have something to say.

5 **Be human.** Get people to know a little more about you – not just the work you, but the whole of you.

6 **Be on message.** Talk around your area of expertise. Let the golden thread shine through your message so it's clear to those that follow you what you stand for and where you play.

7 **Be polite.** Say thanks to those that follow and share your stuff. And 'remember your ABC – always be crediting.' (Hat tip to Charles H Green for this one.)

With so many firms staking a claim on social networking sites, the question you should ask is: Why should folks pay attention to you? It's obvious that valuable content is the key.

Mel Lester, The Business Edge @mellester

The people who are best at social media follow valuable content principles. They aren't pushing sales messages; they are the ones that are engaging with their audience and peers. Social media channels aren't noticeboards where you stick up a postcard advertising your cut-price products; they're a place you meet, chat and share. Social media doesn't really work for corporations with a complicated party line to tow. Where it performs brilliantly is for businesses that trust their people to speak for themselves.

It's really important to remember that you need to be a person as well as a business to get the most out of social media. Yes it is a publishing and distribution tool, but it's a very human place. So, if someone in your network tells you their dog has died, for example, do respond with something personal. Had you learnt that information around the water cooler you wouldn't respond by pressing a sales brochure into their hand and walking away. You'd say you were sorry. It's just the same on Twitter or LinkedIn. It sounds obvious, clunkingly so, but you'd be surprised how many people fall down at just being plain nice.

Valuable Tip

Twitter is a bit like a chat in the pub – you wouldn't hand out sales catalogues and you wouldn't bore people by only ever talking about work all the time.

Twitter wins work for Rachel Goodchild's creative business

Rachel Goodchild attracts over 40 per cent of her new business through Twitter:

You need to be able see the bigger picture where online networking sites are concerned. Remember that at the end of the day you are attempting to drive traffic to your website. Twitter friendships can be built by taking the time to read other companies' Tweets, you will learn something you never expected and you will gain good, strong company links and opportunities. By being interested in others, in return they will be interested in you. Don't put yourself above others and don't boast about the amount of followers you have. Instead post interesting Tweets and be yourself. If done correctly Twitter can be a valuable tool for marketing yourself and your company.

See **www.rachelgoodchild.com** @rachelgoodchild

Vary the content you share by platform

The rules listed earlier apply to all social networks, but the difference between the networks means you need to approach the content differently for each platform. Each has a subtly different style and tone:

LinkedIn updates are more business-like than my Twitter ones, and that feels right to me. I Tweet a lot, and don't want to fill up people's LinkedIn timelines with chat. LinkedIn is like a forum. Twitter is like a cafe.

Sharon Tanton

Here are some valuable content tips for the three major social platforms.

How to be valuable on Twitter

How do you get started? What do you talk about? Just exactly what do you say? What kind of content works best?

How to get started on Twitter

Fill in your Twitter profile completely. You have about three seconds when people check you out so make sure you write it well. Select a good icon or image. Photos work best for a personal feed. Professional shots are best of all. Include a link to your website or blog. This is vital if you want to be trusted on Twitter.

Valuable tips for your Twitter profile

Keep it short and sweet. With only 160 characters to play with, you need to get to the point fast. Make your Twitter biography focused on how you help your clients, rather than a dry summary of your experiences. It's fine to add a bit of personal detail, if you want to attract followers who share your interests outside work. Include a good photograph – vital on every social media profile.

Your profile is complete and you're ready to go.

- **Find people to follow.** Connect with others who you find interesting, people you know, clients, organizations you rate, authors, commentators in your field or journalists you admire.

- **Follow back.** If people follow you and they look interesting, follow them back and see what they've got to say.

- **Be polite.** Thank your new followers in a Tweet, acknowledge those who mention you or 'retweet' your posts.

Tweets

Sarah Smith @StressFreeHR   1hr

"Are you planning a family?" 10 questions never to ask when interviewing. Read our guide to stree-free recruitment http://bit.ly/xyz

Bob Brown @BobBrownLtd   30m

RT@StressFreeHR 10 questions never to ask when interviewing. http://bit.ly/xyz Wish I'd read this when interviewing last week!

- **RT, @, #, DM?** Get up to speed with Twitter lingo. Learn from Twitter's glossary (**http://business.twitter.com/basics/glossary**).

What to write about on Twitter

Once you've got 'hello world' out of the way, then your blogs are a good place to start.

Your first Tweets should be wrapped around links to your blog articles, like this:

For Valentine's Day – why writing good copy is like writing a love letter. bit.ly/eE0L0H – seven tips to improve your business writing.

This Tweet includes a shortened link, a headline hook, and promises a quick read. You can share other people's content in the same way, with a link, and a brief comment about why it's good.

Valuable Tip

Shorten your URL links. Bit.ly is good. You'll have more space to play with, and be able to track the traffic each link brings to your website. Or use Tweetdeck which will shorten the links automatically.

If other people like your content then they'll retweet it, so thank them. Or they might ask you questions about it, in which case engage in conversation.

Tweeting about what you're doing is good for building a useful picture of what you do for potential clients and customers. Obviously 'off to teach accountancy crash course in City' is better than 'cleaning out the bottom of the fridge', so keep it professional. Add 'What are you up to today?' to encourage people to engage with you, and stop your stream from sounding too 'me, me, me'.

- **Stay focused** – Tweet about the issues that matter to your clients/customers. Direct people back to the blog on your website to deepen your connection.
- **Don't sell** – stick to sharing valuable content – yours and other people's.
- **Engage** – respond to questions from others; and ask questions too.
- **Be yourself** – you can be human and relaxed, and admit to walking the dog and drinking coffee.
- **Referrals** – if someone needs help, introduce them to a specialist you might know.

Valuable Tip

Remember that saying something on Twitter is the same as yelling it out on national television. While you're finding your feet steer clear of controversial topics such as religion, politics, sex and other hot topics. The stronger your views, the greater the likelihood of someone taking your Tweets out of context and causing you public embarrassment.

Twitter stops Yoke having to cold call for business

Before we started our company we were worried we might have to cold call to get business. We weren't looking forward to this I can tell you! Then we noticed that many of our potential customers were on Twitter. What has really surprised us is that just by connecting with them on Twitter and swapping news and useful articles was enough to pique their interest. The 'Twitter handshake' is amazingly powerful – you get a totally different response to a cold email or call. You can really build relationships via Twitter and for us those relationships have led to profitable projects.

www.thisisyoke.com @thisisyoke

How often should I Tweet?

Show up regularly, every day is best (weekends are optional). We recommend to our clients just starting out on Twitter that they should aim for at least three Tweets a day:

- one that offers up their own content;
- one that shares somebody else's;
- one that's part of a conversation.

Once you've got into the swing of it you'll find conversations starting all over the place, and you can choose to join in those that interest you most. Many people Tweet far more than that because we see great value in it, but that's how we started, and it's how you can too.

Valuable Tip

Keep an eye on your @ connect feed. It will show you who is connected with you, or mentioned you on Twitter. Respond to these promptly – at least once a day.

Should I schedule my Tweets?

It's a personal tool, so is automating some of your Tweets OK? Once you've built up a bank of content you can use Hootsuite or other online websites and brand management services to publish your Tweets at regular intervals – so you can be publicizing your content even while you're asleep. It's great for building your online presence, but remember that Twitter is a *social* network so don't overdo it. If people like your content, they'll want to engage with you, so you need to check in regularly to pick up conversations, thank the retweeters and respond to comments. Automating the process can be a good use of your time, but make sure you're still there too, having real conversations and connecting.

Valuable Tip

Automated Tweets will almost always be spotted as being impersonal, so as a guide, you would want 90 per cent of your Tweets to be real and human.

How to be valuable on LinkedIn

With over 100 million registered users, it's a very well-used social media platform in the business world. If you're referred by a contact, then LinkedIn is one of the first places people will look to find out more about you.

LinkedIn is the most formal of the social media channels we use. (We imagine most people wearing ties and suits on LinkedIn, whereas Twitter has much more relaxed and eclectic dress code!) Bear this in mind when writing content on LinkedIn.

Use the power of LinkedIn status updates

Your status update is the place to tell the world what you're up to, along with links to your blog articles, and links to other content that you like and that is relevant to your connections. Your profile is visible to anyone who is searching for you specifically by name, or as part of a more general search for people who provide your service (eg communications manager, HR professional, IT security expert).

You have more space to play with than on Twitter, and it's easy to upload links to blogs or videos:

- Links to blogs that answer the kinds of question clients ask you work well on LinkedIn, as they do on Twitter.

- If you've invested in some deeper content – white papers or industry guides for example – then LinkedIn would be an excellent place to promote them.

- Thought leadership-type articles thrive here; it's more heavyweight than Twitter.

How often do I need to update LinkedIn?

A couple of times a week is enough. There are some really valuable discussions happening all over LinkedIn, so make time to keep up and join in.

Should I link Twitter/LinkedIn/Facebook so that one update goes to all channels?

No. It is possible to do this and it would certainly save time but tempting as it may be we'd strongly advise that you treat each social media platform differently.

Valuable content and LinkedIn groups

LinkedIn groups are extremely useful. They build new connections and, if you share the right content in the right groups, can lead to new business.

> I found Sonja via the Bristol and Bath Marketing Network group on LinkedIn. I'd asked a question about website content and she gave me a very helpful answer. This started a discussion and led me to refer her to my client. I've now recommended her to several other clients too.

Tim Chater, Managing Director, Future Drinks Company Limited

Join the LinkedIn groups most relevant to your line of business and share your ideas and content.

NB: This doesn't mean name-dropping your blog at every opportunity. Remember the valuable social media rules – be valuable, not self-promoting. Leave a comment if you think it will add value to the group. A sales message in a group discussion will hit *all* the wrong notes. This is not the place to sell.

Your LinkedIn profile (and how to write it well)

LinkedIn makes it easy for you – just fill in the spaces with all your contact details, your previous experience, and some testimonials, and you're away. That's a good start, and lots of people leave it there, but they're missing out. Past experience and recommendations are important, but what can really sell you is the summary and specialities section. Not filling these in is like going to a party and sitting in the corner not speaking to anyone. This is your chance to answer 'and what do you do?' in the most compelling way, so give it some thought. As much thought, we'd suggest, as you would your website home page. And in the same way that your home page should demonstrate how you help your clients, make it clear here how your experience solves clients' problems.

Five ways to write a better LinkedIn profile

1 **Make it clear about the kind of projects you're looking for.** There's no harm in being upfront, and it makes it easier for potential clients to find you. Using the keywords your clients will be searching for gives you more chance of being found.

2 **Tailor your experience to fit the kind of work you want to be doing.** LinkedIn works best when you treat it as more than an online

CV, so pull out the details that are relevant to projects you'd like to have and add them to strengthen your case. But...

3 **Be succinct.** Think in headlines rather than essays.

4 **Think about clients' needs first.** A section on 'How I can help' makes your profile stand out.

5 **Keep it up to date.** LinkedIn profiles are easy to edit.

How to be valuable on Facebook

What kind of content works on Facebook?

People don't really go onto Facebook to learn, but to be entertained, and to socialize. This is your most human of human faces – it's not your professional face (LinkedIn), and it's not the same as Twitter.

Because it's geared towards entertainment, you need to share things that are funny, beautiful, or inspiring.

Retailers can share up-to-date shopping information, and create a community of customers. Take a look at Boden's Facebook page. The online fashion shop has created a stream, which mixes information from them about their products – previews of new collections etc – with customer photographs and testimonials – look at my daughter in the new jelly-applique T-shirt. A big bank of loyal fans means the page feels full and buzzy. Customers swap stories: '*I just love the breton stripes.*' '*Me too!*' And ask questions: '*Why do so many of your summer dresses have side zips?*'

Oxfam spread the word on Facebook

Facebook has a less frivolous side. Campaign groups can have a very successful presence here. Oxfam, for example, shares some really valuable content through its Facebook page: videos and blogs from volunteers, 'Meet Jodie: Jodie Sandford, 38, is a mum of two and works full time as an IT manager in Barnsley. She has supported Oxfam with a monthly donation for many years and is keen to see how her donations are used,' along with pictures of how your money is helping projects all over the world as well as information on charity events. Lots of interaction and inspiration around a serious message. If your business has a mission, sharing thoughtful, lively and well-produced content that demonstrates how you make a difference can really rally support.

Valuable Tip

Learn from Oxfam. Tell a story through your Facebook content. Break videos into instalments to keep people interested. Leave people wanting to know more!

Facebook helps Endurancelife to build their brand

Endurancelife is an endurance-sport business based in South Devon. Set up in 2003 by a group of friends with a passion for challenge, adventure and the natural world they are quickly becoming a global lifestyle brand.

Their marketing centres on their Facebook page. In one year they have gone from 0 to 15,000 fans with around 100 new ones signing up each day! The aim is to build a global community of endurance sports enthusiasts. They want to inspire more and more people to challenge their limitations, explore the world through endurance sports and experience a better way of life.

Facebook spreads awareness of their brand and is building a passionate community that attends their events and buys their products. The total number of participants in Endurancelife events has doubled in the past year. Marketing manager Andrew Barker shares what works for them:

> With our Facebook posts we make sure we're never overly commercial. We hate being bombarded by commercial sales messages ourselves so why would others engage with a message that is just sell, sell, sell?

> We use Facebook to deliver value to our tribe of enthusiasts. We provide a space where people can talk about endurance sports and share stories amongst people who understand and are equally excited. We post photos, run competitions (they are always popular), share videos, training tips and occasionally promote upcoming events too. We are keen for it to be a really encouraging place for our community.

> We find that Facebook advertising works well in conjunction with our Facebook fan page. We've stopped any other forms of advertising – magazine advertising was too expensive and didn't get us results.

> Facebook has helped us to massively improve our customer service and saved us time and money – most questions are answered for us by tribe members themselves!

> To build a big Facebook following you need to unite people behind a wider mission. I think that's why Facebook works so well for us.

For Endurancelife sharing valuable content on Facebook is the centre of their marketing world and it's getting remarkable results.

How often should I update my Facebook page?

Once a day is fine, as long as what you post has value to the readers.

Valuable tips for your Facebook profile

Adopt a conversational tone. You'll have space for a short 'About' which will appear under your business name, a longer 'description' and 'general information'. Keep it light, and focused on your clients. What will they gain from following you on Facebook? Upload your logo, and add photographs: Facebook is very visual.

Take action

- Join LinkedIn if you are not already there. Update your profile if you are.

- Join Twitter if you are not already there. Connect with us at @sonjajefferson and @sjtanton. We would be delighted to show you how it works.

- Decide if Facebook is right for your business, or try Google+.

Further reading

The Financial Times Guide to Business Networking: How to use the power of online and offline networking for business success, Heather Townsend, Pearson Education Ltd, 2011

The Secrets of Social Media Marketing, Paul Gillin, Quill Driver Books, 2009

Google+ for Business: How Google's social network changes everything, Chris Brogan, Que, 2011

CHAPTER 6
KEEP IN TOUCH WITH ENGAGING EMAIL NEWSLETTERS

Stay in touch. Too many businesses chase new business when existing customers and contacts are far more valuable.

Mick Dickinson of Buzzed Up Marketing www.buzzedup.co.uk @mickdickinson

In this chapter:

- The importance of keeping in contact.
- Email newsletters the valuable way.
- How to build an engaged mailing list.
- An alternative way to keep in touch – autoresponder emails.

Social media will help to keep you front-of-mind, but to really magnify your marketing efforts offer your contacts the opportunity to sign up to your mailing list and communicate with them regularly with a valuable newsletter. Keep in touch with them until they are ready to buy, or buy again.

Printed newsletters work well but can be costly and time-consuming to produce. Email is a more cost effective and very powerful way to automate the process of keeping in contact, if you do it right. This chapter shows you how to build an engaged mailing list and keep in touch with valuable email content to help you win more business.

The importance of keeping in contact

Not everybody is ready to buy at the first contact. Research suggests that only 2 per cent of deals are struck at a first meeting. The other 98 per cent only happen once a certain level of trust has been established. Contacts that don't turn into sales straight away are often forgotten but this could be opportunity lost. If your company Christmas card is the only time old contacts hear from you each year then you are missing out on business. Contrary to a popular myth, marketing is not just about generating new leads. Effective marketing nurtures existing relationships too. As one of our favourite US marketing bloggers puts it:

> *So many businesses think 'marketing' is the same thing as 'lead generation'. In other words that marketing equals chasing down strangers so you can wrestle them through the conversion process and turn them into customers.*
>
> Sonia Simone, Copyblogger **www.copyblogger.com** @copyblogger

Many professional businesses devote all their time and a considerable amount of budget to lead generation when there's a far more cost effective and rewarding way to boost sales. Professional Services business development consultant Ian Brodie (**www.ianbrodie.com**) makes the useful analogy that some companies treat marketing like a one-night stand. They pour all their energies into pursuing the next big contract; finding out everything there is to know about their prospect so they can say the right things to impress at a pitch, but then moving on straight away if they don't win the work. Or they finish the job as fast as they can and never look back.

Instead of leaving in a cloud of dust use your knowledge and creative energies to build trusted relationships over time. Be patient. If you keep in contact regularly in ways people appreciate and find useful they will reward you with their business.

Keeping in touch with valuable content means your customers and contacts continue to receive information they value and can learn from. You get an opportunity to build relationships, prove your expertise and stay in contact, so they'll remember you when the need arises. A win:win all round.

Email newsletters the valuable way

Email is still a very powerful method of communication, with current and future customers. E-newsletters – or e-zines as they are sometimes called – automate the process of keeping in touch. Despite the overcrowding of our inboxes they *will* be read and acted upon if the content they contain is valuable enough to the reader. Do it well and it is a great way to turn contacts into customers, and motivate customers to buy again.

How it works:

- You build a database by inviting people to join your email mailing list.
- You create an email newsletter using an email marketing tool (try **www.mailchimp.com** to start).
- You send a regular communication to your database by email.
- These usually include engaging articles, and news linking to content on your site and others.
- You distribute this weekly or monthly.

Make sure you include valuable content

When people keep in touch with you by sending emailed promotional offers, you just know that they don't really care about you as a person. Even the 'friendly' newsletter that gives a front page 'Employee of the Month Profile' offers nothing of value to you. So remember the valuable principles and hold off on the self-promotion.

You won't keep friends very long if all you do is send generic 'what we've been up to' email updates. (Ask yourself how much you look forward to receiving round robin updates: *'This year Gemma got straight As in her A levels and the family was lucky enough to enjoy a wonderful walking holiday in Tuscany.'* We'd bet you don't love them that much.)

Make your e-newsletters helpful rather than salesy, packed with advice, not advertising, and focused on your client's business needs, not your business wins.

You will know if your emails contain valuable content. How? Well, the current recipients will stay with you and those people with forward your email to their contacts, so your mailing list will grow through referrals. The more valuable the content, the greater this multiplying effect!

Mel Lester and his very valuable email newsletter

For an example of a monthly email newsletter that works, take a look at Mel Lester, A US-based business consultant we first connected with via Twitter. He produces one of the most valuable, targeted newsletters we've seen to date. The content he shares is always relevant, interesting and useful. He doesn't go overboard on graphics; it's straightforward, simple, and full of information that his target market wants to read. You can read it at a glance, but it's easy to explore more of the bits that really catch your eye. It's full, without feeling overwhelming or overloaded. It gets Mel great results.

Sign up to Mel's fantastic newsletter at: www.blog-bizedge.biz

Five qualities your newsletter needs:

1 clear aim;

2 authenticity;

3 voice;

4 relevance;

5 simple but effective design.

Integrate your newsletter with the rest of your content. Link back from stories in your newsletter to your website. Having an edited version of the story in your newsletter for the time-pressed is a good idea, with a link to your website for the fuller version. We don't always what to click to read more, so make sure your newsletter has integrity in its own right. Archive old newsletters on your website so they can be found by potential clients, and by Google.

> **Valuable Tip**
>
> Add your Twitter, Facebook and Google+ links to the email newsletter, to let people easily connect with you in whatever way suits them best.

Three different types of valuable content newsletter:

- The blog article round-up: wrap up your recent blog articles in a monthly newsletter communication. This is the easiest form of e-newsletter to deliver.

- The themed newsletter: pick a topic and deliver the best information from you and other sources.

- The laser focus newsletter: pick a topic and go into it in depth in your monthly communication. More work but seriously valuable content on one subject each month.

How to build an engaged mailing list

People rave about 'targeted' lists. I'll take a warm community of people who feel seen any day over 'targeting'. (Sure, maybe this isn't the best way to sell, but I don't write emails to sell. I write emails to connect and be helpful. If I'm selling you something, it's because I think it'll help.)

Chris Brogan, Human Business Works **www.chrisbrogan.com** @chrisbrogan

For email to be effective you've obviously got to have a list of interested people to talk to, but how do you get one? What you don't do is buy one and spam information to everyone on the list. In today's quickly changing job market there's a very high chance you'll be buying out-of-date information so the person you're targeting will already be working somewhere else. Building a list takes a combination of research and putting the valuable content marketing principles into action.

Get people's interest by telling them what they are signing up for, like this:

Sign up to receive free monthly business marketing tips, tactics and valuable resources via email by subscribing to the Valuable Content online newsletter **www.valuablecontent.co.uk/newsletter**

How to motivate more sign-ups

- **Ask existing clients to opt in.** Makes sense to start with the people you already know.

- **Make sign-up easy.** Joining up your blogs with your website via social media should get you a stream of interested readers who like what you say. As well as a retweet button to help them share your valuable content with their followers, include a sign-up to your newsletter. Make it really easy for people to subscribe with a clear and accessible sign-up form. Not one that pops up in your face as soon as you land on the site – they're a real turn off – but one that's easy to see, and promoted alongside your incredibly useful blog.

- **Use an ethical bribe.** You can use your valuable content as a lure for newsletter sign-ups. The promise of a free download written on key subjects will tempt some people to want to hear more from you. (Make sure your site has lots of absolutely free valuable stuff too.)

- **Promote your list widely.** Whenever you meet people or speak to new contacts, in the real world as well as online. We invite every new Valuable Content contact to opt in with an automated invitation each month.

- **Cross-promote.** Encourage sign-up from your Facebook account, your G+ page, and through your Tweets. Engaging headlines that offer little snippets of the stories can tempt people to sign up and read more.

What is spam, and how can I make sure I'm not sending it?

Spam is unsolicited and unwanted junk mail, almost always for products or services that you don't want, and so often coming from overseas companies you have never heard of. You will never be at risk of sending this if you have followed the guidelines in this book:

- Always ask people's permission to email them.
- Give the recipient an easy option to unsubscribe.
- Only send information they will find valuable.
- Any sales pitch or special offers constitute less than 5 per cent of each email message.

Being asked for, and delivered from a trusted source will ensure your email marketing gets through, but there's still a chance it can feel like spam if it's written in the wrong way. Write it without a real reader in mind, and it won't hit the target. Fill it with sales messages, and it might as well be a pharmacy ad. If it's useful, people will remember it, and keep hold of it until the time comes to contact you. If it serves no purpose, you might as well not send it in the first place.

An alternative way to keep in touch – autoresponder emails

Autoresponders are an automated email marketing technique that is handy to master if you want to convert more contacts into leads. Autoresponding is the process of writing and scheduling automatically sent emails to contacts who have signed up to your list. Autoresponder email sequences are an underused lead generation tool for many of us in the business world and, if written well, a great example of valuable content in action.

Make it personal, like John Jantch

I use an autoresponder to reply once someone subscribes. I send an evergreen issue of my newsletter so they get a taste of the value right away. A few days after they subscribe I also send what feels like a much more personal thank you note from me. This is a text email that is very simple and tells them I am glad they subscribed. I get constant feedback from people that, while they may know it's not really a personal note, love the personal feel. I suggest you adopt this approach.

John Jantch *Duct Tape Marketing* **www.ducttapemarketing.com** @ducttape

Autoresponders are a way of leading potential clients to the information that will be most valuable to them, and converting interest into sales. They can be part of your email newsletter campaign, as described by John above, or as a way of targeting different sections of your audience.

If you have more than one niche, autoresponders are a useful way of addressing your different audiences. They can feel more personal than newsletters, and can guide people through the maze of things you know towards the bits they are most interested in. Good email autoresponders confirm that you're in safe hands, and that you've come to the right place.

You really need to give away valuable content, almost like mini tutorials.

Lee Duncan educates and inspires with autoresponders

Business coach Lee Duncan, author of *Double Your Business*, uses autoresponders with great results.

I have used autoresponders for several years now. As a business coach I've been encouraging clients to use them for even longer to increase the number of leads coming in.

My goal with every email is to offer some robust insights that my type of client can use to improve their business. It's my aim to educate and inspire in a practical and valuable way. For example: how to improve cashflow through better credit control; why giving employees shares doesn't motivate most of them; why business grinds to a halt when the owner goes on holiday.

Six months after I first put this autoresponder sequence into play my coaching client base had more than doubled! I often get messages of thanks back from readers and they will respond to particular messages with queries about how I can help them to solve similar issues in their businesses.

Lee Duncan, *Double Your Business* **www.leeduncan.com** @lee_duncan

Tips for planning your first autoresponder campaign

- Aim – what do you want to achieve? How many more clients? Be specific.
- Focus – what part of your service will be most useful to your target market?
- Write – create a series of five emails that take your target reader by the hand through the process.
- Promote – on your website, via social media, let people know exactly what problems and issues you are able to solve for them.

Take action

- Put together a list of your existing contacts for a newsletter list.
- Think about the newsletters you subscribe to. Which do you read and which do you ignore?
- Would your clients appreciate a monthly round-up of your blogs, or a shorter 'one key message' type of communication?

Some newsletters to inspire you

Sign up to the valuable newsletters of these companies for more tips on business development, content and web marketing:

www.copyblogger.com

www.bryonythomas.com

www.hingemarketing.com

www.trustedadvisor.com/trustmatters

www.principledselling.org

www.humanbusinessworks.com/newsletter

CHAPTER 7
GET SEARCH ENGINE SAVVY

None of your website's elements matter if nobody comes to your site. The heart of a high performance website lies in its search engine authority. You will rank well and gain consistent traffic. From keyword research and implementation to link building, SEO is a long-term initiative that all high performing websites must tackle.

Sean McVey, Hinge Marketing www.hingemarketing.com

In this chapter:

- Why you should care about search engines.
- What search engines want.
- Top five ways to optimize your content for search.

If you want to maximize your investment in valuable content, learn to care about search engines. Search Engine Optimization, or SEO as it is called, is a huge topic but there are a few simple techniques that every business can employ to get more people to find your content on the web. Here's what you need to know (and nothing more).

Why you should care about search engines

There are various ways to get people to your website: you can tell them about it, giving them a link to your URL; you can entice them there by sharing links to useful articles on social media sites; you can share links back to your site in your email newsletters; you can write a blog so valuable that people willingly refer it to their contacts. Do all this and you *will* get visitors to your website. If your content is valuable enough when they get there you'll build their trust, generate a lead and ultimately win their business. But if you want to maximize your investment in all this content you need to get search engine savvy too.

SEO is what you do to make your website and content as search engine friendly as possible so you can get it in front of people who are actively looking for it on the web. Your aim is to get to the top or near the top of major search engine results pages for the terms you want to be found for. If you create lots of valuable content *and* properly optimize that content for the search engines you increase your chances of getting found and boost traffic to your website. Getting to the top of the search engines results pages means you get found by the people you want to find you.

SEO has brought Hinge Marketing a massive leap in leads

At Hinge we have always created valuable educational content for our clients and it has consistently brought us good results. But when we started taking search engine optimization seriously a couple of years ago we saw a massive leap in inbound leads. We used to get about 10 per cent of our leads through the fresh content we posted on our site. With our new focus on keywords we now get over 70 per cent!

Sean McVey, Online Marketing Manager, Hinge Marketing

What search engines want

Creating high-quality content for your site is by far the most important thing you can do when it comes to SEO. Adrian Knight of Digital Investments UK explains:

Google's mission is to serve the highest quality and relevant material to its searches. Help them to do this by producing high quality, valuable content created with the user in mind, and you will do well.

Adrian Knight, Digital Investments, **www.digitalinvestments.co.uk**

Modern SEO is all about creating content so valuable and compelling that other people naturally want to promote it, to share it, like it and Tweet about it. The more that other people link to your site, the more of an authority Google and the other search engines will consider you to be on the subject, doing great things for your ranking.

Valuable Tip

'Try to make a site that is so fantastic you become an authority in your niche', says Matt Cutts, Head of Google's Web Spam Team

Learning SEO in depth, in order to be able to implement every element within your content marketing, takes a lot of time and a lot of dedication. Luckily there are plenty of things that the average content creator can do in order to make a website more accessible and give it a greater chance of being found by your target audience.

You'll find more help on writing content that search engines will find, and people will like in the chapters on writing, but for now, here's what you need to know to start shaping your content, and creating a website that pulls in leads for your business.

Top five ways to optimize your content for search

1 Keyword research.

2 Update meta tags and content.

3 Inbound links/outbound links.

4 Update with regular content.

5 Share your content.

Keyword research

Choosing the correct keywords is the foundation to your success with SEO. Pick the right ones and your rankings will rise, get it wrong and you'll see little results, no matter how well you do in the other stages. Do your research; you will gain a clear view of the words and phrases people most often use when thinking about and searching for your topic online. You can learn how to speak their language, allowing you to create content to satisfy their needs, which is exactly what search engines are looking for.

To generate relevant keywords first talk directly to your customers and find out why they come to you. Then use Google's free keyword research tool (adwords.google.com/select/KeywordToolExternal), which allows you to observe the keywords and phrases that people have actually used to find information online in the past.

Advice from expert SEO copywriter Louise Nelhams

The first and most important element of SEO is keyword research – while there are plenty of highly complex ways to identify the best keywords to use, the Google Adwords tool is a good enough starting point for the inexperienced. Look at search volumes and competition levels – however appropriate you may think a keyword or phrase is, if nobody is using it as a search term, then it's simply not worth including. During your keyword research, it's also a good idea to undertake some competitor analysis; look for your biggest competitors and take a look at the page source on their web pages. This will allow you to identify the keywords that they're using in their metadata and help you to optimize your web content more effectively.

Once you work out the best keywords to use, you need to decide which pages to use them on. If you've got a fairly expansive collection of potential keywords, try to target one or two on each page.

The art of crafting keywords

With keyword research you are making data-driven decisions – the data is dictating which keywords you should target. Now that you've decided on the keywords you want to use on each of the website pages, you need to think about how you're going to incorporate them into the copy for the best effects. Usual practice for a copywriter is to keep the content as succinct as possible – we tend to want to avoid wasted words. However, it's generally believed that every page needs a minimum of 400 words in order to be indexed properly. This means lots of research and a good relationship with your client; you need to make sure that every page is original and offers something different to the other pages on the website.

By carefully targeting your keywords you are more likely to answer the search query effectively or 'own' the search, allowing you to get to the top of that search results page. Don't be too scattergun – keep to within 5 to 20 keywords for your site.

Louise Nelhams **www.advancedwritingsolutions.co.uk** @AWS-copywriter

Updating meta tags and content

We mentioned that Google needs a bit of spoon-feeding. To feed it correctly you need to set your 'metadata' right (there's one of those off-putting technical terms we mentioned at the start!). Think of metadata as data about your data, or information about your content. It just means acting like a good librarian and labelling your content correctly so search engines can find you easily. Include your chosen keywords – this is a way of saying to the search engines, 'Hey! Look at me! This page is relevant!'

- **Page titles**. Use your keywords in your page title. This is the blue link that appears on the Google search page. Keep it short – up to 72 characters will be visible. Convince the searcher your content is relevant. This is your meta tag, crucial when optimizing for search.

- **Meta Descriptions**. 165-character summary of your page or article using key search terms. This is what appears on Google's search results and it needs to be informative, relevant, interesting and succinct. This is 'prime advertising space' so make it compelling enough that someone will click on your link and not your competitors. Also, include the keyword(s) you're targeting.

- **Headings**. Important for the reader scanning your article or page, and for Google too. Use them to show what the page is all about. These are called H1 tags – they're important so include keywords.

- **Images**. Google can't read an image so help it by labelling the images you use. This is called the Alt Tag. Again, include the keywords you're targeting.

Valuable Tip

If you have a blog or a website with a content management system, ask your developer to set it up so you can set the metadata yourself for each new page or article.

Inbound links/outbound links

When the search engine 'spiders' enter your site, you want them to stay there as long as possible so that they can find all the wonderful content that you have in there. To do this, it is important to ensure that you don't have any dead ends – there should always be links to other pages within your site, particularly those that hold related information. Link intelligently in and out of your site. The more links there are to a page, the more the search engines will think it is important.

> **Valuable Tip**
>
> Optimize your links by using your keywords within the link text – this is called 'anchor text' since it anchors your web page to the keyword.

It is also important to link to other relevant websites. If you write an article that draws information from and links to a host of other relevant sites, the search engines consider that you're an expert on this subject and will place more importance on your website.

Update with regular content

The search engine 'spiders' that crawl around the web looking for information do keep a check on your website – they return periodically to see if you've modified or added anything. Google, like us, isn't so keen on stale content – freshen it up every so often, by adding to your blog for example.

Share your content

What other people have to say about your content is more valuable from a search (and people) perspective. Getting your content onto other sites, particularly on well-respected and popular sites will really help when it comes to your search engine ranking. This point cannot be stressed enough.

The rise of blogging and social media has revolutionized how search engines rank websites. According to Copyblogger a huge 85 per cent of the total factors that influence search engine rankings is dependent on what happens off your site on other websites and social media platforms across the web.

Fall in love with social media and share your content all over the place and Google will reward you. Provided your content is high quality and valuable enough, the more you share, the more you will generate links back from other sites.

> ### Valuable Tip
>
> Ask the other sites that house your content if they will include your target keywords in the anchor text. Vital if you are trying to rank high for a keyword.

You will find more tips on writing for the web in Chapter 13 and a useful glossary of SEO terms in the Resources section at the back of the book.

Take action

- Use Google Adwords' keyword research tool to investigate the keywords customers use to find services like yours.
- Look back over your previous blog posts. Have you included keyword-rich headings? If not, add them now.
- Check that you're labelling your content for search engines. Ask for help from an SEO expert if you need help to get you on the right track.

Further reading

(For beginners) *Search Engine Optimization, an Hour a Day*, Jennifer Grappone, Gradiva Couzin, John Wiley and Sons, 2011

(More advanced) *The Art of SEO, Mastering Search Engine Optimization*, Eric Enge, Stephen Spencer, Rand Fishkin, Jessie C Stricchiola, O'Reilly, 2009

CHAPTER 8
YOUR VALUABLE WEBSITE

For a new visitor to your website, you have less than three seconds to make your best impression. For existing or returning customers, there are on average 40 other business like you trying to grab their business away, almost at any cost. Your online web content is your differentiator, your personality, your message and your offer. It's the ink on your banknotes, the art on your canvas.

Richard Dennys, Chief Marketing Officer, Qype www.qype.com

In this chapter:

- The role of a good business website.
- More library than online brochure.
- Traditional website vs valuable website.
- Guidelines for a valuable website.
- Think content first (before you get the web designers in).
- Instructions for your web designer/developer.
- Ideas for key sections of your site.
- Tips for writing the content on your website.

This chapter shows you how to make your website valuable to your customers and turn it into a fully contributing member of your sales team.

The role of a good business website

Your website is the base for all your valuable content, and the heart of your business communications. Every piece of content you create – your blogs, downloads, videos and case studies – needs a place here. Potential customers and clients will be led to your website from all directions so you need to make it clear to them that they've come to the right place. Your website should feel like home to them. *Here's a place where people really understand me.*

Just like the blogs you are writing need to start with the questions your customers are asking – their concerns and problems – your entire website needs to embody the same customer-focused attitude. Yes, the website is about you, and your business, but it needs to be written and designed from the customer's point of view. Not *this is what we do* but *here's how we help you.*

The role of a good website is to engage web visitors with your business; to pull them closer to you, get their trust, inspire them to spread the word about you, and to buy from you when the time is right. A *valuable content* website is a powerful tool for pulling in leads, and converting them into sales. Because you're asking a lot more from your website than a standard site it needs to be designed differently. You're building a library of content that's going to expand over time, not designing a one-off brochure, so you've got to think bigger. Getting the balance right between engaging people in your message and converting their interest into action is the key.

Designing a valuable website is a specialist job. This chapter explains the priorities for a good website. It will give you some guidance so that you can engage the right web team to create a site that pulls in leads for your business. This advice will save you time and money. Far too many companies waste resources on websites that just don't work for them.

In his book *A Website That Works,* Mark O'Brien of niche web development consultancy Newfangled is very clear on the three goals for a business website:

1 to attract prospects;
2 to get them to the areas of the site they are most interested in;
3 to bring them into the next level of their relationship with the firm.

This chapter shows you how to create a website that does just that – one that is genuinely useful to your target readers and exceedingly beneficial to your business.

More library than online brochure

Many company websites are no more than flat, online brochures. This is perfectly fine if all you want is a credibility tool. But if you want to engage visitors and generate leads from your website – a regular stream of qualified, inbound leads – then you need to do more than just present basic information on your company.

Remember that not all visitors will be ready to buy straight away. The majority will be much earlier in the buying process – scouting for information for when the time is right. As well as details on your company and its products or services you need information that hits home with those who are just browsing. Help them to solve the challenges they face, build a relationship with them and they'll remember you when the time comes to buy. To achieve this, turn your website into a valuable hub of information and resources your customers and potential customers can delve into and learn from – more library than brochure.

Payplus turns its website into a resource hub and draws in leads

Payplus has turned its Payroll Services Centre website into a powerful, lead-generating machine by packing it full of high-quality, valuable content that educates and informs buyers of their services. With over 100 pages of payroll-related information on the site plus a regularly updated blog they have shot to the top of Google rankings. It's getting them found on the web for payroll-related searches.

> From their home page: *'The Payplus Payroll Services Centre is the place to come for information and resources about payroll. It's a hub for all things payroll related: we'll unravel the jargon, answer your questions, and tell you all you need to know to make sure it runs smoothly in your organization.'*

The Payroll Services Centre website provides value in advance of a sale. Their website is written, designed and structured around the needs of their clients. It includes highly relevant pages, articles, testimonials and downloads for their different target audiences, such as school payrolls. By helping to answer their visitors' specific questions they gain their trust and motivate people to get in touch. The website is generating over 60 good leads a month.

See: www.payroll-services-centre.co.uk

> *The valuable content approach really works. Within two months of launching our new website we saw a massive uplift in visitors, inbound leads and sales. It has literally doubled our business.*
>
> Paul Marsden, Payplus @payrollsc

Valuable Tip

When it comes to getting leads from your website the trick is to get the quality vs quantity balance right with your content. A quantity of any old content won't do. It has to be relevant, helpful and compelling to the people you want to do business with.

Paul Marsden, Payplus

Valuable websites have many more pages than a slimline brochure – they attempt to answer every client question. More pages mean more useful information for the visitor, and more fodder for the search engines to index too. With all this content on your website, the organization and structure of the information becomes key. Make it simple for the visitor to find what they want. Smart user-centred design is a must.

Traditional website vs valuable website

What elements make a traditional brochure-style website different from a valuable content website? Here are a couple of different layouts to show you what we mean.

Characteristics of a traditional, brochure-style website

1 **All about the company.** Menu doesn't even mention the customer. Nothing valuable on the site to help clients solve their HR challenges.

2 **No clear message.** No clear story for the customer, just a meaningless image. Customer can't easily see what is in it for them.

3 **Self-oriented wording.** The copy is all about the company and how great they are. Plenty of nonsense gobbledygook too.

4 **Generalist.** Trying to be everything to everyone (and catching no one in the process).

5 **Selling, not helping.** Sales brochure is the only download. Presumes that visitors want to buy. Nothing useful to take away if you are browsing and not yet ready to buy. Not generous.

6 **Company news.** Internal-looking news of no real interest to the customer, and out of date.

Characteristics of a valuable, lead-generating website

1 **Created for the customer.** The whole website is designed and written around the needs of the customer. Valuable content is prioritized.

2 **Clear message.** Sets the scene and gives a good picture of what this company is all about and what it will do for them.

3 **Customer-focused wording.** Engages with their issues and tells them they are in the right place.

4 **Niche.** Not for every business. They can laser in on the needs of a focused market.

5 **Engaging, helpful content in a variety of formats.** Covers all requirements.

6 **Deep content.** Helps to establish you as an expert in their eyes.

7 **Monthly newsletter** to maintain contact and build relationships.

8 **Highlights case studies.** Still important credibility-builders today.

9 **Good balance.** Mix of information about the company and helpful content.

10 **Blog articles.** Lots of fresh, useful content. A hit with customers and search engines alike.

11 **Is this you?** Gets the customer to information that's relevant to their challenge, fast.

12 **Makes connections.** Links to social media where you can make contact, build the relationship.

13 **Need for search function.** Because there's so much great content on the site you need a way of finding it!

A traditional website is like a virtual pat on the back for yourself; a valuable site is like putting your arm around your customer, helping them to do business better. A valuable website is far more engaging.

James Jefferson, Unity Information Systems **www.unity-is.co.uk**

Guidelines for a valuable website

Clear, consistent messaging is the starting place for any good website. What is the story you want to get across? The visitor needs to see very quickly whether they are in the right place and understand what you do. Include a descriptive strapline for the business, clear 'what we do' text on the home page, and in the 'About Us' section – wording that describes your offering, with jargon-free copy and consistent tone throughout.

Valuable, lead-generating websites talk about the target visitor and their needs and challenges as much as they do about the company. Don't make the website all about you. This is the number-one mistake people make with their sites. Provide content that is written to meet *their* needs.

What many websites forget is that not everyone coming to their site wants to buy from them. Most people are earlier in the buying process. **Prioritize the valuable content.** Gather together all your existing content: your blogs, collect your case studies, archived newsletters, videos, podcasts, past presentations – all the useful pieces of content you've created to help your clients. Links to the valuable content you have created should take pride of place on the home page of your website, and promoted wherever they are relevant throughout the rest of the site. They're your most powerful engagement and conversion tools, so make sure they're in prime position, the stars of the show. *Along with client-focus, this prioritization of valuable*

content is the key thing that differentiates a valuable content site from a standard website. Keep the good content coming. Adding fresh content, regularly, will show that your website is alive and give visitors a reason to come back. Search engines rate sites with fresh relevant content.

People frequently design a website first, and then tack all the content on afterwards – words are seen as just a filler to replace the lorem ipsum text, blogs are an afterthought hidden at the back of the website. By spotlighting your valuable content, and designing the website around it, you'll create a far stronger and more useful website.

Carefully design the site around the visitor's needs so they can find the information they need fast. Remember that every page is a potential entry point to your site. If someone searches on the web for a key phrase you rank highly for, they probably won't land on your home page. Write and design each page carefully, knowing that someone might land on it without having seen any other page on your site.

Integrate blogging, social media, email 'keep in touch' marketing and search. A standard brochure-style website keeps itself to itself. Unless you give someone the URL (website address), you'll be lucky if your clients find it in a search. A *valuable content* website makes links with the world through shared content, social media and smart SEO. It's more visible, out there, easy to find and connected.

Conversion elements

A good site is a balance of useful and sales content. The purpose is both to draw people in to building a relationship with your company, and motivate them to buy from your when the time is right. **Clear calls to action across the site are key.** You've got their interest. What do you want people to do? Because people will be arriving at your website via your blogs or from any number of places, every page needs to have a clear call to action. Make it obvious what you want people to do next. Action is everything when it comes to your website. The key actions you want people to take when they visit the site are:

- Get in touch.
- Keep in touch – sign up to your updates or newsletter.
- Take something away – download a document they find useful.

Include these calls to action as relevant in the sidebars and footer at the end of each page. Give calls to action some emotional weight by showing you understand the client's problem. 'Wrestling with end of year accounts? Call Sarah', is better than 'Call us'.

Sidebars are your friends. On a valuable website you have a library of content, and sales pages that talk about your company and the products/ services it provides. Connect the two by signposting the reader to related content in your sidebars. Use them to direct people deeper into the website and get the visitor to stick around. 'Our Services' is a key place where your valuable content can add richness, authority and depth. In addition to a clear description of how you help, signpost people towards a relevant case study, or your most recent blog article, or a handy download. Make it easy for them to get to the information that they need.

> **Valuable Tip**
>
> No page should be a dead end; every page should open a door to further useful and engaging content.

Think content first (before you get the web designers in)

Your website is a work of commerce, not a work of art.

Mark O'Brien in A Website That Works. **www.newfangled.com**
@newfangledmark

If you are thinking about designing or redesigning your company website, it is tempting to focus on how it should look to impress your customers. This strategy prioritizes form over function, aesthetics over information. It's an easy trap to fall into. Design agencies can dazzle you with the importance of 'messaging style', 'corporate identity' and 'brand personality'. '*It's all in the design*', they say. But this design-led approach fails to consider how and why people buy your services and what customers want from a professional business website.

Design is very important, but if you concentrate on colour schemes before planning the content you run the risk of creating a great-looking site that customers either have no use for or cannot use.

> 'With a few exceptions, people visit the web for its utility, not its beauty. Having a visually appealing site is good, of course, but content is golden',

Web usability guru Jakob Nielsen **www.useit.com**

Before you pick up the phone to a web designer, think very carefully about what you and your customers want from your site; what does it need to say to convince them to buy your services and how should this content be laid out?

A good way to get this clear is to create a 'wireframe' for your website. Wireframing is a powerful web planning strategy that helps you construct a successful business website.

Planning your website

- First work out what *you* want to accomplish with your website and what customers you want to attract.

- Ask your customers what they want from their visits to your site.

- Work out what search terms they would use to find your site.

- Identify what each part of the site needs to do and what it needs to say to respond to your customers' requirements.

- Build your 'wireframe': a non-graphical layout of each page of your site. This will enable you to organize the content and test the layout *before* you start building the site.

Draw out a structure with pen and paper, or use a simple wireframing tool like Balsamiq (**www.balsamiq.com**). If you wireframe first, before a single graphic is chosen or line of code written, you have a far greater chance of web success, for you and your customers, and you'll avoid expensive and time-consuming revisions at a later date.

If you are thinking about investing in a new business website, place content at the heart of your project. First think what you and your customers want from your site. The colour scheme can wait.

> **Valuable Tip**
>
> Spend as much time planning your new website as you do building it.

NB: You will find a useful website content checklist in the Resources section at the back of the book to help you with your planning.

Instructions for your web designer/developer

Now you're clear on what you want the website to do, it's time to talk to someone who can build it for you. Most website suppliers are good aesthetically or technically, however not all fully understand the business needs and functionality their clients require. Use this checklist to guide your web designer on your requirements.

> **Valuable Tip**
>
> Hire a web designer/developer who creates valuable content for their own business. This way you'll know that they understand your requirements.

Tell your designer that you will need:

- **A fully content managed site.** CMS platforms such as Wordpress or Drupal make it very easy to add and update pages of additional content. You'll be constantly updating the website so you want to be able to do it yourself.

- **A content-centred site** rather than a highly visual experience. Any movement, sounds, graphical devices, blocks of imagery should fulfil a specific purpose.

- **Simple, intuitive navigation and layout,** designed around target visitor needs. It must be very easy for people to find the information they want.

- **Integrated, fully functioning and well-designed blog(s).**

- **An engaging home page** that prioritizes valuable content and pulls people in.

- **The ability to upload, store, highlight deeper content easily** – video, podcasts and other content.

- **Search engine fundamentals** – a logical URL structure and the ability to set metadata (see Chapter 7).

- **Analytics** – you want to know who's coming to your site, what pages are your most read, what's working and what's not.

- **Engagement tools** – eg social share buttons, ability to comment on articles, enquiry forms.

- **Integration with an email-marketing tool** so visitors can sign up for content updates.

- **Ability to show related content on every page.** No page should feel like a dead end – there's always more to discover.

- **Strong visual design** – professional and interesting but uncluttered.

- **Professional page and content layout** – paying attention to typography and styling to help the content stand out.

- **Mobile-friendly** – to leave a positive impression with mobile users too.

- **Search capability.**

- **Clear contact details.**

Valuable Tip

Ask your web designer to read this chapter so they can understand the level of linking, the depth of connection, and the volume of content your website needs to house.

Ideas for key sections of your site

Home page

Although people will arrive at your site via lots of pages, you still need a well-designed home page that encompasses the following:

- Clarity of purpose.
- Clear navigation.
- Is this you?
- Valuable content loud and proud.
- Room to breathe.

Your home page should make people feel at home – understood, looked after, in the right place.

About us

Potential clients will want to know what kind of company you are, so this section is Important. It's a mistake to think they just want to know about you though; they're really after information that tells them what problems you can solve and if you are the kind of team who can help them:

- See the page from your potential client's point of view. Your team's golfing prowess might be awesome, but how does that help? Focus here on your approach to the business.
- Share your mission. What do you believe, and why? Define your audience – what kind of people can your business help?
- Don't write too much. Remember the rules of good web writing. Short and to the point is good. Strong headlines will draw people in, so link to further pages if there's more to say.
- Make sure the whole page links well to the rest of your site. Relevant 'About Us' copy will make natural links to your clients, services and case studies, so embed them in the site.

Our people

Apart from figuring out if your approach to business inspires confidence, potential clients like to see who they will be working with:

- Good professional photographs of the team are a must.
- Show some personality, although still remember that potential clients are most interested in themselves and their concerns so don't go overboard with personal stuff.

- Quick Q and As are an engaging way of getting across enough information to show your human face without becoming a bore.
- Pull people further into the website – Conscious Solutions'. 'Fact or Fiction' is a neat approach. (**www.conscious.co.uk/site/people/profile/dgilroy**)

About you

Define your customers or clients and their concerns in an engaging way. This is the place to demonstrate how well you understand their problems, and show how you can help them overcome them. Direct different potential buyers to the relevant resources and services with some well-crafted 'Is this you?' copy. You'll probably have more than one service, and several different types of buyer, so create 'about you' copy for each key sector.

Define each problem, and offer answers. Watch this video, read this blog, download this free guide. We're down to the details of how you can help them, so get your valuable content sorted, and on display.

Case studies and testimonials

Don't tell me the moon is shining; show me the glint of light on broken glass.
Anton Chekhov

In a low-trust world, we crave independent evidence from real people. There is huge power in hearing your story from the perspective of those who have been on the receiving end of your products or services. It's much more believable coming from others than it is from you.

Case studies are particularly important when potential customers are evaluating you as a potential partner to work with. Buyers will have a whole lot of questions and a good case study helps to answer them. They set your services in context and when targeted right will mirror the buyer's situation. Good case studies draw in leads, increase sales to new and existing customers and garner support for your business and ideas.

Customer stories serve a role that no other promotional tools truly fill by accomplishing the three purposes at once: credibility, education and validation.
Casey Hibbard, *Stories That Sell* **www.storiesthatsellguide.com**

Here's how to make your case studies work on your website:

- **Spotlight your client.** Don't shout about yourself, put the client you worked for centre stage. Write the case study from *their* perspective. Describe the client's story not your own and you'll end up with a powerful marketing tool.

- **Make the client look good.** Show they made an intelligent decision in using you. Talk about their successes, not your own. This has the added benefit of making your clients feel good – good for customer loyalty and goodwill in your direction too. The best case studies are a joint promotional tool for both you *and* the client, and a valuable aid to potential clients looking to go down a similar route.

- **Show how your product, service or organization solved a specific issue.** Frame the business problem you solved clearly and upfront. Make it part of your case study headline.

- **Give value.** Make this type of content really valuable by giving away learning points for others to follow. This is the way to really prove both your expertise and usefulness, and to make your case studies a coherent part of your whole valuable website, and valuable content in their own right.

- **Involve the customer.** Traditionally, case studies can be technically accurate but dry. To give them more impact, instead of just presenting facts and figures, involve the customer. Add the human element for an engaging story. A lot of marketing tends to be making things up in a vacuum. How do you know what benefits a client got from working with you? You will only find out if you ask!

Valuable Tip

At the end of every assignment or sale ask your client for their feedback. What did they really think? Why did they hire you? What were the real benefits of your involvement? What did they appreciate and what could you do better next time?

- **Embed case studies into your business process.** Interviewing every client once a project is over can become part of your quality assurance process, as well as a source of valuable marketing material – a powerful quality assurance, customer service and business development tool.

You will find a case study template in the Resources section at the end of the book.

Our services

The 'services' section is the real nitty gritty of what you do, and these pages can be the most difficult to write. If your business sells technical services, for example, there is a risk they can become stilted and jargon-filled, distancing your potential clients. If you have a number of services for a wide variety of clients, your website can become confusing.

Integrating your services pages with your blog, case studies and testimonials is a great way round this. Demonstrating your approach in action for real-life companies shows you doing, rather than just saying.

You need a brief but clear description of your services for the people in the early stages of web research. Remember to phrase your services answering the question 'How do you help' and not just 'What do you do'.

> *'We help small to medium-sized firms in the Thames Valley make the most of their IT – help desk support, IT investment, and IT for business development' is better than '10 years of IT support – you can trust us'.*

Write a short, clear overview, and signpost to more pages that look at individual services in more detail, and to relevant valuable content that backs up your credentials – white papers, case studies and the relevant blog articles.

You need more detail on your services to satisfy readers who want to dig deeper into how you could help them. If your potential clients expect a high level of technical detail, now's the time to get it in, but marry this with links to further valuable articles written in a conversational tone that demonstrate your company in action.

Write a detailed page for each of your services, tailoring the call to action to the most common problems you know clients face in this area. And while we say detailed, we mean a maximum of 400 words, with the copy broken down into manageable chunks, and scaffolded with keyword headlines to make the page easy to read at a glance, as well as in more detail.

Useful structure for service copy

- Name of service.
- Who this is relevant for.
- Why they need it/what problem it solves.
- What your service involves.
- Benefits.
- Relevant image/photo/video.
- Case studies.
- Customer testimonials, if any.

Go deeper. Add sub pages under each service that answer different clients' specific questions about that service area – great for meeting client needs and for Google too. Link to related content on that subject around the rest of your site – to case studies, to relevant articles, downloads. Remember to add clear calls to action – tell the reader what you want them to do if they are intersted in what you have to say.

Free resources

Call it what you will – resources, free stuff, knowledge bank or library – this is an important section of your site. Your valuable content will be highlighted throughout the website, wherever relevant, but it needs a home of its own too. Showcase the valuable stuff in one easy to find place. Gather together your articles, newsletters, videos, podcasts, downloads and slide show presentations and make them available as valuable free resources for your potential clients.

Just as a library needs cataloguing and signposting, your resources need to be presented so that people searching can find what they want quickly. Organizing your content into categories is important, and linking between connected pieces is the best way to keep people engaged on your site. Dividing by format too makes it easier for clients to access the information in the way they want.

> **Valuable Tip**
>
> This part of your website will grow as you create more and more deep content. Invest in design that makes it look interesting, welcoming and the kind of place people will want to spend some time.

Tips for writing the content on your website

With a designer on board to create the structure of your site, you can either get to work on writing the pages, or engage a skilled copywriter to help you create that content. Here are the principles each page needs to follow.

1. Easy to read at a glance. New visitors will make snap judgements about your site. If you want to connect with them, remove all clutter and get to the point fast.

> *New visitors, especially those from search engines, will not read your content first, they'll scan it and see if it looks applicable to them.*
>
> Chris Pearson, DIY Themes

How to grab the attention of busy readers:

- Highlight important keywords or phrases.
- Use bulleted lists.
- Use meaningful subheadings (not clever ones).
- Only one idea per paragraph.
- Start with a summary.
- Cut down the word count (half or less than conventional writing).

2. SEO friendly. Search engine algorithms are getting better and better all the time but if you don't label your information properly then they are going to struggle to index your stuff. If you're going to get the most from your investment in content, learn what search engines want so that those searching can find your site. Valuable content with good labelling is what search engine optimization is all about. Think like a good librarian and index your stuff appropriately.

3. Client focused. Every page, even 'About us', needs to be written from the client's point of view. How you help, not how great you are. Engage with the reader, set out their challenges, and answer their questions.

You'll find more writing tips to help you with your website content in Chapter 13.

Take action

- Review your current website. Does it pass the customer test at the back of the book? Will it support your valuable content goals?

- If you need a redesign, ask your network for web design recommendations. For inspiration for examples of best practice check out the websites of companies who have won a Valuable Content Award: **www.valuablecontent.co.uk/valuablecontentaward**

- Go to the Resources section at the back of this book and you will find a list of questions to help you complete your website content.

Further reading

A Website That Works: How marketing agencies can create business generating sites, Mark O'Brien, Rockbench Publishing, 2011

The Strategic Web Designer: How to confidently navigate the web design process, Christopher Butler, North Light Books, 2012

See how your website is performing now. Try Hubspot's *Website Grader*: marketing.grader.com

CHAPTER 9
ADD DEEPER WRITTEN CONTENT: WHITE PAPERS, E-BOOKS AND BOOKS

There's a place for shallow, and a place for deep. Twitter is shallow; blogs are deeper. Articles are deeper yet. Or books – books are real deep.

Charles H Green, author of *The Trusted Advisor*
www.trustedadvisor.com

In this chapter:

- The benefits to your business of deeper content.
- Your deeper written content options.
- What deeper content to choose when.
- 10 top white paper and e-book writing tips.
- Should you make people fill out a form to download your content?
- The importance of a strong landing page.
- Great content needs great design.
- Repurposing your stock content.

We look at how to increase the value of your content by sharing educational whitepapers, e-books and printed business books. Find out what to use when, and how to write them for best results.

The benefits to your business of deeper content

We want to introduce you to an important metaphor for your content. The concept of **stock and flow** originates from the world of economics but can also be linked to the production of content.

> *Flow is the feed. It's the posts and the Tweets. It's the stream of daily and sub-daily updates that remind people that you exist. Stock is the durable stuff. It's the content you produce that's as interesting in two months (or two years) as it is today... And the real magic trick is to put them both together. To keep the ball bouncing with your flow – to maintain that open channel of communication – while you work on some kick-ass stock in the background. Sacrifice neither. It's the hybrid strategy.*
>
> Robin Sloan, the Snarkmarket blog snarkmarket.com

We think Robin hits the nail on the head. To market our businesses effectively today we need to commit to both stock and flow content and get the balance right.

To date in this book we've concentrated on flow content. Blogs, short articles and social media updates are your bread and butter content – easier to throw together, easy for people to consume quickly. Sometimes you need to provide something more sustaining – good stock content with more nutritional value and a longer shelf life. White papers, e-books and business books take more time and thought to produce, and they feed people's desire for deeper knowledge. Ten top tips are great, most of the time, but there are times when your customer wants something a bit meatier.

Getting some longer form and more detailed pieces into your content tool kit is really useful. A desire for something more substantial is part of the early stages of researching potential companies to work with, so it's well worth investment. Producing deeper written content is a sound way of demonstrating expertise and authority in your area and creating it makes you better at what you do. It takes you further into your niche, sparking new ideas and making more connections.

This type of content is invaluable for sales people. As you'll learn in Chapter 13, well-produced deeper written content is a way of opening doors, increasing engagement and developing useful new relationships that you can convert to sales: the best business card you'll ever produce.

Five reasons to invest in deeper content:

1 Authority – it shows a powerful grasp of the issues in your field.

2 Invaluable sales tool – it is evidence of your capabilities, and people will share it.

3 More engagement – it pulls more people to your business.

4 Can be repurposed – it gives you fuel for blogs, tweets, videos.

5 Demonstrates your expertise – deeper content really is 'show not tell'.

Because it takes longer to produce, and demands more thought and planning, creating deeper written content isn't a one-person job. Unlike your blogs and Tweets, you'll almost certainly need some assistance. Help with research, help with design, help with editing – if you're planning on upping the ante with deeper content, a team effort will take your content to the next level.

Valuable Tip

'If you share deeper content you'll find that sign-ups to your email list will rocket. We devised a simple marketing planner and offered it as an incentive for people to join our mailing list. We had a 40 per cent increase in sign-ups and three new sales enquires within a week!'

Eli Barbary, email marketing expert at Valuable Content @elibarbary

Your deeper written content options

1 White papers, sometimes called discussion papers.

2 E-books.

3 Published business books.

4 Other formats.

White papers, discussion papers

Positioned somewhere in between a magazine article and an academic paper, these powerful forms of content can supercharge your thought-leadership efforts. They are authoritative, educational reports or guides that show the reader how to solve a particular issue. Especially useful in technical and consultancy fields, truly valuable white papers are widely read and passed on from person to person.

There are many different forms of white paper. Discussion papers are a close cousin but slightly more conversational and less academic in tone (in government these lighter discussion pieces are called green papers). Other flavours include: the valuable guide, the executive briefing, the position paper, the special report, and the research report.

Technology white paper expert Gordon Graham identifies the following key characteristics for all modern white papers:

- a document that contains narrative text;
- includes an introduction or executive summary;
- at least 5–6 pages (1,500 words) long, in portrait format;
- educational, practical and useful, not a sales pitch;
- used before a sale, not after a sale;
- provides facts, not just opinion.

Professional service marketers Raintoday (**www.raintoday.com**) surveyed 730 leaders of professional service companies and asked 'What offers are most effective in generating new leads?' White papers were among the most effective offers, with 28 per cent of respondents rating them very or extremely effective.

Marketing Sherpa finds that 69 per cent of customers who download and like your white paper PDFs will pass it on to a colleague: 36 per cent of those will pass it on to a direct supervisor. 57 per cent of IT purchase decision-makers said that a white paper influenced at least one buying decision in the year.

Valuable Tip

For inspiration and research you can browse a huge library of technology white papers at **www.findwhitepapers.com**.

E-books

An e-book is a white paper turned on its side and made more visually interesting, with fewer words on each page. It is designed to be read on-screen but can be printed out too. Different in tone and style to white papers, they are usually less formal but equally useful to a wider readership. E-books are a great vehicle for spreading your ideas far and wide. They're substantial enough to go into useful detail, not so long as to feel like a chore to read. Emailable, and very shareable with no printing or distribution costs, once you've written an e-book you can quickly get it out to the people who matter to you:

- mix of narrative text and visual content;
- approachable, practical, easy to read;
- answers a key question in your field;
- length varies wildly.

Valuable Tip

An e-book should ideally be readable in 40 minutes – typical commute time within London or New York.

Other formats

Handbooks, guides, manuals, workbooks – get creative. What would your clients or customers value most?

Valuable Tip

'Build up content into something deep and valuable. Write a series of blogs on different aspects of one theme and at the end of the month you can compile a cool, highly visual and easily digestible e-book. Or compile case studies to create a compendium. Manuals to create a handbook. Images to create a showcase. You get the idea.'

Lucinda Brook, **www.marketingclout.co.uk** @lucindabrook

Published business books

If blogs are the kings of valuable content, business books are the Masters of the Universe. Not for everyone, and by no means essential in your valuable content tool kit, but extremely worthwhile for the minority of people who relish the challenge. Consultants and advisors will certainly benefit from writing and publishing a book. A book is a power-charged business card; proof of the credibility of your ideas, and it can allow you to lift your rate as a result of the increase in inbound enquiries.

Whether you get a publishing deal or self-publish, being an author of a published book gives your ideas authority. As Charles H Green, author of best-selling *The Trusted Advisor* explains:

> *It's mechanically very simple to assemble a book but somehow your fame, your respect goes up considerably if you have a book to your name. If you give someone a book it's five dollars of paper and cardboard marked up triple yet somehow it has this patina of 'Oh my gosh, that's wonderful! You gave me a book! Thank you!' People respect it.*

Charles H Green **www.trustedadvisor.com** @charleshgreen

Finance on a Beermat wins business

I can say with certainty that our self-published book has got us sales meetings, and it definitely makes second meetings more productive. If you're pitching in a large company to a lot of people the book will get passed around, people will see the book before they see you. People will sell the book to other colleagues in the department, saying 'this is what we need' so when you get to the meeting people are already on your side.

A lot of business owners that we work with are experts in very narrow technical fields, so they assume what they're going through is something nobody else understands. Our book shows that we do understand their problems and can offer answers. What we're doing in our business, what we sell, is intangible. We are selling ideas; it's not something you can see. The book is a great tangible example of the value that we add. It distinguishes us from other people.

I think I can pass on two big things learnt when I was writing the book. Firstly, it makes you realize how much you know and how much value you can add. The second is you're forced to find a way to convey what you know in a way that makes it easy to understand. It is an excellent discipline; it makes you know your subject matter far more deeply. It makes you find other ways to explain yourself, which in turn makes it easy for you to engage with more people. The words come to you more easily when you have spent time thinking deeply about them, trying to write them.

Stephen King, author of *Finance on a Beermat* **www.f-works.co.uk** @steve_fworks

There used to be only one way of publishing a book, and that was through a traditional publishing house, but that's no longer the case. Self-publishing is now a serious option for any author, shaking off its 'vanity publishing' connotations and producing some really high-quality publications (you will find information on both options on the Valuable Content website).

Writing a book will bring you many business advantages. It is in no way the simple option as any author will tell you, but it's an investment that will bring huge benefit – to you and your business. Is it time you wrote it all down?

What deeper content to choose when?

Which format is right for you? It depends on your content, your business and your customers. Some of the above are only really relevant for those whose products or services require a 'considered purchase', og consultants, advisers, software products, etc. Selling hamburgers or other quick purchase commodities? White papers are not really for you. But there is no reason why you cannot still up the value of the content you deliver. Get creative – recipe books, calendars, interactive games. If you understand your customers well enough you'll be able to come up with content of real value that they'll treasure for far longer than blog or a Tweet:

- Write a white paper if you're in a competitive technical field. Especially good for consultants, getting your message read at board level and influencing a highly educated clientele.

- Write an e-book if you are communicating to a wider field in a conversational tone. Particularly good for social sharing.

- Publish a book if you love your subject, you're an expert in your field, and you know there's a gap in the market for what you want to say. If you really want the stamp of authority, this is the option for you.

Planning is crucial for longer form content

Writing a quality white paper, e-book or book obviously takes more time and thought than writing a blog article but it is well worth the extra effort in terms of the credibility these bestow.

Before you start writing, plan carefully. It will make the paper or book far easier to write, with less rework through the process and a high-quality more engaging read as a result.

> **Valuable Tip**
>
> 'We use mind-mapping software to help us plan our e-books', says David Gilroy, Conscious Solutions

You'll find a planning guide for longer form content in the Resources section at the back of the book.

10 top white paper and e-book writing tips

1 **Pick a subject close to your customer's heart.** Address their problems, challenges and needs, educate them and help by giving a solution.

2 **Write for your reader.** Although a white paper can help to drive sales, it's not an overt sales pitch. Ditch the marketing hype and keep it thoughtful, factual and helpful. It's a matter of style. NOT: 'Company X has done it again! Another great widget to help you overcome your IT security issues...'. BETTER: 'If you are concerned about IT security, a new class of technical products may be the solution you are looking for...'.

3 **Benefits, not features.** Make sure your content passes the 'so what?' test. Tell your readers why your approach matters and what is in it for them if they go down the route you suggest.

4 **Include interesting content.** Interview clients who use this approach, include their comments, case studies, perhaps an historical overview of how we got to this position in the first place.

5 **Back up your approach.** Back up your logical argument with hard facts. Use third party evidence, do your research and reference your sources.

6 **Write in plain English.** Don't baffle your readers with industry gobbledygook. Don't use jargon that will go over the head of your audience.

7 **Include links.** Signpost the reader to other relevant content on your website and motivate them to investigate further, to read more of your ideas, to get to know your business better.

8 **Design matters.** Really it does. Invest in professional layout, design and production to enhance the content.

9 **Write like a journalist – top down.** Get the most important juicy stuff upfront – answer the reader's questions at the start. Get into the habit of summarizing – lead with a summary: get their attention, tell them what you are going to say, then say it. It's a busy world, with lots of content competing for their attention – tell them quickly why they should give up their time to yours? Then follow the traditional beginning, middle, end format.

10 **Get the word out there.** Post it on your website and make sure your readers can find it by putting a link from the home page to the download and creating a carefully optimized landing page on the site. Mail or email it to your clients and prospects. Share it with your social media network. Use it to open doors and start conversations. Include it as a link in your email signature.

Valuable Tip

Use a white paper or e-book to help you open or close a sale. Write one on the subject you are looking to solve for a particular customer. This approach will help you to get meetings, explain your thinking, prove your expertise and win their trust (See Chapter 12).

Should you make people fill out a form to download your content?

Whether or not to get people to complete a registration form on your website in order to download your deeper valuable content is a contentious issue in the world of web marketing.

For many, 'gating' your content by asking the reader to hand over their email address in exchange for strong content is a fair exchange. You are offering something valuable that you have sweated hard to produce. They are obviously interested in your subject, so you want to keep talking to them. Collect their email address in return for your valuable content and add them to your mailing list or to a series of useful targeted emails, and you can 'nurture the lead' towards a sale.

The opposing view is that you shouldn't gate anything you produce. If someone is interested in your content, let them have it and set your content free. They will choose to come back to you and buy from you if it is valuable enough when the time is right. The most important thing is to give them a good experience of your brand.

> *For your ideas to spread... you've got to give up control. Make your information on the web totally free for people to access, with absolutely no virtual strings attached: no electronic gates, no registration requirements, and no email address checking necessary.*
>
> David Meerman Scott, **www.webinknow.com** @dmscott

Most content is freely available on the web now. Video, for example, is probably your most expensive content option, freely available via YouTube so why restrict the rest of your content?

At Valuable Content we are in the no-gate camp. None of the content on our site apart from our newsletter has a sign-up form – it's free for anyone to download, talk about and share, and share they do. We believe that giving generously and freely is the best way to build your reputation and your business. If your content is valuable enough, trust you will get plenty in return. Motivating people to sign up to our list without forcing them is our approach.

Do I ever give my details in exchange for content? Depends on how much I trust the integrity and authority of the information holder. Both increase with the provision of free information.

Stephen King, F-Works, **www.f-works.co.uk** @steve_fworks

You will need to weigh up the pros and cons for your own business. If you gate your content you will create a database of interested people that you can add to your mail, but you'll lose a proportion of potentially interested customers who will click away once they reach your electronic barrier.

If you do decide to gate your content make sure it's only for the really, really valuable stuff; exceptional content – detailed surveys, unique studies, or really useful guides that can't be found elsewhere on the web. You have to earn the right to ask for people's email addresses in a world where inboxes are already overloaded. So your gated content better be worthwhile.

Valuable Tip

If you gate your content make any sign-up fields as straightforward as possible. The fewer fields, the more likely people are to fill them in. A 20-field form to fill in will turn away all but the most doggedly determined.

The importance of a strong landing page

To motivate people to download and read your deeper written content you will need a compelling pitch or 'landing page', where you convert that spark of interest into the action.

Here are five things to avoid with your landing page:

1 **Dull headline**. They're interested but that interest could easily evaporate if the page doesn't live up to its promise.

2 **Too much clutter**. Your blog post feed and lively sidebar is a distraction here. Just give them the information they want.

3 **Too much choice**. You only want them to do one thing – sign up – so get rid of anything else on the page.

4 **Bad design**. Don't lose your head and start jazzing the page up with loads of colour and fancy images. Keep it clear and professional.

5 **Over-estimating your audience's interest**. We're all lazy, too lazy to even scroll down a lot of the time. Get your message across quickly in the top half of the page.

Valuable Tip

The best landing pages are clear, focused and economical. Good sales copywriting is key.

Great content needs great design

As wordsmiths, you might expect us to argue for the supremacy of the written word. But the deeper we go into the world of valuable content, the more strongly we realize the inseparable link between content and design. The greatest words in the world won't get read if the design is all over the place. The smoothest design in the world will trip up if the words don't make good sense.

Lizzie Everard, one of our favourite graphic designers (she created the illustrations in this book) puts it well:

> Flashy, superfluous and self-indulgent design that exists for itself is like having a Prada handbag filled with cheap cosmetics. But brilliant, well-crafted words and insights that are not dressed for the party will miss all the fun.

Lizzie Everard **www.lizzieeverard.com** @lizzieeverard

Commit to quality. People won't take your words seriously if they're not professionally presented. And they will be equally disappointed if your design makes empty promises. If you are investing in creating deeper content, don't forget to invest in some great design too.

- Use good-quality photographs or illustrations that augment, not distract, from your words. Ideally, it's a partnership.

- Good typography really helps communicate the hierarchy of your information. Think: 'Where do I want people to look first?'
- Expression, character and consistency in design can make your brand's personality shine.

Repurposing your content

Once you've put the time and resources in longer pieces of content there is a lot you can do with them. The material you gather for a white paper or e-book, for example, can fuel lots of smaller blog posts, case studies, videos, webinars. Repurpose your deeper content to squeeze maximum value from it.

One white paper or e-book can become:

- 10 blogs;
- 50 short tips on Twitter;
- a short series of guides;
- a slideshow;
- shared graphics on Pinterest,
- a targeted email marketing campaign;
- the basis of a webinar;
- a series of podcasts;
- a video.

The thinking and writing that you do for your deeper written content can be stretched and tweaked in many directions, to fit the needs of different audiences and the styles of specific social media channels. It's well worth the investment.

Take action

- Identify 10 topics about which you or your company could produce white papers. Ask your sales people for ideas.
- Identify two of these for consideration to be e-books rather than white papers.

- Ask the salespeople whether there are any topics about which clients have said, 'I wish there was a video on this topic?'

Further reading

Writing White Papers: How to capture readers and keep them engaged, Michael A Stelzner, WhitePaperSource Publishing, 2006

The Insider's Guide to Getting your Book Published, Rachael Stock, Trotman, 2011

Articles on our site: www.valuablecontent.co.uk/category/business-books

CHAPTER 10
DIVERSIFY WITH DIFFERENT FORMATS – VIDEO, AUDIO AND MORE

Communication should never be a sales pitch. People want authenticity. Video is a hugely powerful way to tell stories. If you do it well, people love it.

Mark Sinclair, yourBusinessChannel www.yourbusinesschannel.com

In this chapter:

- Different formats to connect with more people.
- The rise and rise of video content.
- Where to start with video.
- Working with a video company.
- Wonderful webinars.
- The power of infographics.
- Podcasts for business.
- Online games as sales tools.
- Mobile Apps.

The right words will get your message across, but written content isn't the only way to connect. Think about the smart infographic that says it so simply, the video that captures the sense of a person more quickly than 50 words could do, the podcast you can listen to on the train. Making your website truly valuable means embracing many different ways to communicate. It means getting your message into different formats to inspire, guide and educate your website users; making it easy for people to get to your valuable stuff, in whatever way suits them best.

We are all now used to receiving content in a wide variety of formats. And there are myriad different options today – fuelled by new technologies that make it even easier for you to connect with customers and clients in engaging ways. In this chapter we cover video, webinars, podcasts, infographics and online games but there are more and more options coming through; endless possibilities to get your message across. Mix it up, play around with them, have some fun, see what you can create.

Different formats to connect with more people

However good your writing, sometimes there is a better way to say it. Some people find it easier to grasp information visually; others find it easier to listen to something to get a sense of a subject. Not everyone will want to read your white paper, or even your blog. Understanding that different people have very different learning styles – seeing, hearing, doing – is a useful way of making sure you're giving your business message the best chance of a warm reception.

Valuable Tip

Give people the chance to access your message and content in whatever way suits them.

It's also good housekeeping to try to connect in different formats. Try to get the most value from every piece of content you create by reusing your content in different formats. Cross-referencing case studies and blog posts, creating downloads from guides, recycling stories we've used before with minor tweaks to keep them relevant. Video, audio, webinars are more tools you can use to get the most out of what you're doing. If you were giving a talk, it would make sense to get professional help to film it or record it. The 50 people in the room listening to you swells to an unlimited number of people who will be able to hear what you're saying, via the content on your website. Imagine: you can still be talking to potential clients while you're lying on a beach somewhere!

Of course, valuable content principles apply to new media formats as tightly as they do to the written word – only the highest quality will do.

The rise and rise of video content

Video content adds another layer of richness, credibility and accessibility to your website. YouTube dominates web usage, and is a fantastic business tool. Instead of written testimonials, why not use 25 seconds of your client talking about how you've helped them? As a change from a written blog, why not put up a film of you and a colleague discussing the issue? Don't just link to high-quality white papers; show your clients the way to films of great lectures that are relevant and inspiring.

A good video will get more people to your website. A study by Aimclear shows that people are more likely to click through to a website if the search throws up video results:

> Videos in universal search results have a 41 per cent higher click-through rate than plain text.

Aimclear **www.aimclearblog.com**

Aimclear's research video encouraged people to stick around longer (on average two minutes more on your website). Longer visits aren't just good news for keeping people interested in you and your business, they give you extra SEO oomph too. Google is placing more value on longer visits, so anything that encourages visitors to spend more time on your website will improve your ranking.

Google ranks 'informational' videos most highly, which is just the kind of content that any business can produce well. Approach video content in the same way as written content: produce something useful and you'll please both your clients and search engines.

Instant rapport

Video is great for capturing your approach and giving people a real sense of you as a person:

> At a sales meeting recently the new client said 'I've watched your videos on the website so many times I feel I know you already.' They were already part sold before the meeting even started!
>
> Bryony Thomas Clear Thought Consulting **www.bryonythomas.com** @bryonythomas

As a way of breaking the ice, and starting to build rapport, video helps enormously. Establishing trust is a crucial step in the sales cycle, so something that gives potential clients a genuine sense of you – your voice, your way of speaking, your style – should be embraced. If your personality is absolutely key to your business success, and particularly a business where potential clients might be nervous of working with you – say divorce lawyers, driving instructors, or dentists – a video can be an excellent way of showing what you're like, and helping people get a powerful impression of what it would be like to be with you.

Emotional connection

When someone visits your website for the first time, you're aiming for a fast emotional connection. Your content needs to be factually accurate, but it's also got to feel right. We all make judgements on a whole heap of factors, some of them sensible – *that's the information I was looking for* – and some of them less easy to categorize – *that font irritates me. I don't like that picture. That colour reminds me of horrible Auntie Joan.* Video can cut through this fast, taking your viewer straight to the heart of what you're saying, with less chance of petty distractions pulling their attention away. Straight talking, hearing a voice speaking sense, seeing someone smile and look relaxed, all of these start the process of emotional connection and can be achieved quickly through the right video content.

Woolley and Co Solicitors' video gives potential clients what they want

Teresa Harris, at Woolley and Co, UK family law solicitors explains why they created a series of videos on divorce for their website.

Our website gets a lot of traffic, and there's a lot of content there. We're good at blogging and producing written material, and we've created a huge bank of articles, but we know that sometimes it's difficult to absorb that amount of text. Not everyone likes to receive information that way. We wanted a way to bring the material to life, and we saw video as another way of getting our message through to potential clients. Divorce is the area where we get most enquiries, so it made sense to create some video content that would answer the questions people have around this highly stressful area.

We worked with a specialist video company and shot seven films in a day, which you can find on our website and our YouTube channel. They're very simple films, just one of our solicitors talking as they would during a first meeting. We cover some of the most commonly asked questions around divorce and children, divorce and finance. The most popular one is 'How to get a divorce' followed by 'How to save money on your divorce'.

They work very well for us; clients appreciate them. People are nervous about talking to a solicitor, divorce is a difficult process, but the videos show our human side. It puts your mind at ease when you can see the person you'll be talking to, and hear the way they speak. It makes a first meeting easier.

Video is an important part of our marketing mix. For us, blogs serve a different purpose – they're good for profile raising, increasing our search engine ranking, demonstrating our expertise and the fact we're up-to-date on current issues – but our blog readership tends to be our peers and the media. The videos are firmly focused on what clients want to know. Different people like their information in different ways, you need to do it all ways for the best results.

Teresa Harris, Woolley and Co Solicitors, **www.family lawfirm.co.uk**

YouTube's guidelines for 'compelling content'

You can use YouTube and create your own channel, like Woolley and Co has done. There are lots of ways to build a community around it. Have a look at the different styles people have used and work out the one that looks like it will work for you. Here are a few ways to create interesting videos and interact with the potential clients on YouTube.

- **Direct Dialogue.** Make videos that create a dialogue about problems and issues that customers have. Ask questions and solicit video responses.

- **Tell Serial Stories.** Engage viewers with a series of videos that tell a story around a specific theme, and keep them coming back for more. Once you've created a few episodes, visit your playlist page and create a new playlist. This allows you to develop several video narratives targeted at particular demographics.

- **Use Endorsements.** Whether they're from celebrities or people you've helped, it's good to have supporters chiming in about why your work matters.

Expert advice from Mark Sinclair of yourBusinessChannel

yourBusinessChannel is a YouTube partner that has logged 1.7 million views over the last few years. It works with big brands like Blackberry, organizations like the London Chamber of Commerce and Industry as well as numerous smaller businesses who want to get their story across in a direct and engaging way. Founder Mark Sinclair is convinced of the power of video to help businesses connect with customers, influencers and clients. Mark keeps a keen eye on heavyweight studies measuring the impact of video.

The statistics speak for themselves:

- Video is 98 per cent more likely to put you on the first page of a search engine.
- Forbes Insight found that 59 per cent of senior executives prefer to watch video instead of reading text, if both are available on the same page.
- Video in email marketing has been shown to increase click-through rates by over 96 per cent.

   'Video marketing has really taken off over the last 18 months. It's powerful because it's easy to consume, instant, audio and visual, accessible, flexible, and people love it. If you're looking for a way of getting your message across with impact, we'd say 'try video'.'

See **www.yourbusinesschannel.com**

Where to start with video

The possibilities of filmed content are huge, and it can feel a little overawing. More and more corporations are weighing in with high production value films; the news is full of videos that have gone viral – some amateur, some corporate – making real money for the film owners. Serious businesses are investing heavily in video content, so how can you possibly compete? How do you start?

Video content ideas that won't break the bank

Unlike blogging, which just needs you and a pen, video content has a higher initial financial outlay. The possibilities of filmed content are endless – you could recreate *Inception* as a metaphor for the changing business world, if you had the time and the budget. Your entire office could dress as characters from *Downton Abbey* to make a point about your traditional levels of service. (Perhaps a bit much, although we would very much like to see them, and predict they'll be big viral hits.)

It's possible to make good video content without a big budget.

Simple stuff that works

- First-meeting videos – you talking, just as you would in an initial client meeting. Good for ice breaking.
- 'How to' videos – explanation, screen grabs.
- Filmed conversations – you and a colleague talking together on an issue close to your clients' hearts.
- Presentation videos – film of you giving a client-friendly presentation.
- Testimonials – talking heads of your clients.

Dan Roberts' 200 personal training videos do the work

London-based personal trainer Dan Roberts shares fantastically useful video training tips on his YouTube channel. *How to get rid of a beer belly at home* anyone? Or perhaps, *How to get rid of your saddlebags?* Over 300 other websites feature his videos so Dan gets a lot of free publicity. Dan's videos get him found on the web, quickly build trust and set him apart from the crowd. Larger fitness and training firms can learn a lot from his valuable video content – as a one-man band Dan has presented 200 short videos in total. Perhaps one day someone will approach him to set up franchises everywhere!

See **www.danrobertstraining.com**

Valuable video checklist

Video making is an art and we recommend you engage a local crew to do the technical side. This will leave you to stay on top of the message, and the content of any dialogue. If you're confident of doing it yourself, follow our checklist – the 'keep your feet on the ground' bottom line in creating video content for small businesses:

- **Make it relevant.** Ask yourself, what question is this film answering? What story is it telling? How is this helping my clients?

- **Keep it short and to the point.** Choose one topic and stick to it. Better to make five short and succinct videos than one long and rambling one.

- **Make sure people can hear it.** Wonky audio is a real turn off. Invest in a decent microphone, or hand over production to a professional team.

- **Think about lighting.** If you don't have a lighting kit, position your subject near the best light source available. If you're filming in a room with a window, stand with your back to it to avoid the silhouette effect that occurs when your subject is positioned between camera and sunlight.

- **Hold tight.** Use a tripod if your film doesn't involve any moves, invest in a grip if you're filming a sequence with a hand-held device. (You'll find more useful tips at **http://fitzternet.com/2011/06/6-tips-and-tools-for-better-web-marketing-videos/)**

- **Make sure it works!** Can it be viewed on PCs and smart phones? Faulty links frustrate, so test before spreading the word.

Working with a video company

Video production is an area where lots of small businesses are happy to ask for outside help. There are lots of great companies around, and they'll lead the creative side of the production. The key thing for you to remember is that you want a video that will be useful to your clients. There is no point in investing your entire marketing budget in a big glossy advertisement for your business. Remember, everyone skips the adverts. If you want potential clients and customers to watch, create something that interests them, and answers their questions. Make that clear to your director when you're explaining what you want to achieve – it's not 'a film about us', it's a 'film for our clients'.

How to get the best out of your video company

- **Be clear** – know the key message you want to get across and assemble your ideas into a storyboard.
- **Give them lots of background** – tell them about your customers, your business, and the unique way you help.
- **Do your research** – point them towards content you like, and tell them why that approach feels right for you.
- **Be open** – making a video is a chance to try new things, so be flexible and prepared to go out of your comfort zone.
- **Practise presentation with a webcam at home** – get used to saying it out loud, sing it in the shower, bore your kids with it!
- **Set aside enough time** – you don't want to have to rush on the day, so clear the decks for the time your producer suggests.

Do I have to appear on camera?

The reticence many people feel about committing their thoughts to writing can be increased hugely when it comes to speaking on camera. *I'll look awful, I hate my voice, I'm too embarrassed.* Well, yes, perfectly natural, but get over it. Video is such a wonderfully direct way to connect with people – for them to get that real sense of you that's so important for establishing trust – that it pays to embrace it. Of course, video content on your site doesn't have to feature you – you can interview clients, tell stories about products, share other people's ideas that will strike a chord with your audience – but if your personality is key to your business success (if you train people, teach, lead groups) then it's really worth getting to grips with filmed content.

Ann-Marie McCormack, a film director at AmmAFilms makes videos for companies to use on their websites, and has dealt with many people who feel nervous at the thought of being filmed. Here are her tips to help you relax.

Valuable tips for being at ease on camera:

- Just be yourself. Wear something you feel confident in and don't act. Be natural.

- Be reassured that it is not live. Only 10 per cent of what is shot is generally used, so if you don't like what you have said, it can be cut out and you have control.

- Focus on chatting directly to the interviewer and ignore the camera.

- Remember the camera crew and interviewer are there to make you look good and feel at ease, so relax and let them do their job.

- If you feel you didn't get what you wanted to say across, you can do it again... and again... and again.

Wonderful webinars

Webinars are another non-written tool that businesses can use to connect with clients, and demonstrate all-round valuable usefulness. Good webinars generate leads, and raise your reputation – perfect valuable content fodder!

A webinar is a seminar conducted over the Internet. It is a great chance to connect with a range of people and teach them something useful. A workshop without the expense of hiring a huge meeting room, connecting with people worldwide, all without leaving your chair. Business coach Louise Barnes-Johnstone recommends them because they are more engaging than blogging or connecting on social media.

> *Webinars engage more of the senses. People are Seeing, Hearing and Doing all at the same time, so absorb new information more fully. If you're trying to get across a lot of detailed information and you want people to understand your message, a webinar is the next best thing to being there in person. When you want to connect with people who are in different geographic locations, webinars require no travel time or fuel costs.*

Louise Barnes-Johnstone, SimplyBusinessCoaching.com @louisebj

Valuable tips
- Thoroughly prepare what you want to cover and test the webinar software before the big day. Do a trial run of the entire presentation to friends or family to familiarize yourself with all the controls.

- Send out plenty of reminders beforehand, up to and including the day itself. It's surprising how many people leave it to the last minute to register, or lose the log-in details.

- Get there early (at least 15 minutes) so you can test the audio etc and greet people. Display a 'Holding Slide' until the event starts.

- Record it and create new content for your website or blog. It's also good feedback for you!

- Introduce yourself and say why you're qualified to talk about the topic. Don't launch straight into point 1, give people a chance to settle down.

- Give great, high-value information and don't oversell (if you are selling something).

- Follow up after the event.

As with every tool, sharing valuable content is the key. We'll leave you with this advice from Roland Millward, founder of the Online Social Media Bootcamp:

From the very start you need to capture your viewers' attention. The content of the webinar must give the attendee something of value, teach them something new or inspire them in other ways. Add value by inviting industry experts to share some great information on the webinar. Have some photos, slides and videos that can be used to add interest.

www.profitsrgood.com

The power of infographics

Information portrayed graphically, instead of in pure words or numbers, can say a huge amount in a small space. It appeals to people who prefer visual over verbal explanation, and opens up your message to more people. Check out 'Information is Beautiful' (**www.informationisbeautiful.net**) to see how big ideas and thoughts can be expressed succinctly with creative design.

If you have a complex idea to get across, a lot of figures to express, or processes to explain, it might be worth speaking to a graphic designer and commissioning some clever visual representations instead of relying on straight words and numbers. Your brief to the designer should include: *'Make this really easy to understand'... 'I want people to see what we do straight away'... 'I want it to look stylish and add value to my website.'*

'Infographics' have become a very popular form of online content, much shared on social media sites.

RSG's infographic gets a warm response

Recruitment firm RSG commissioned research into perceptions of their industry. The study turned up some fascinating statistics that the business wanted to share with candidates, clients and peers. Rather than present the information as a white paper, they chose to create a well-designed infographic and share it online.

Designer Oli Corse explains:

> I know from experience that there's just so much information and data on the web that it's hard to take it all in. It's hard to concentrate on it, let alone engage with it. The infographic was a way of making all that data visually appealing. For infographics to really work they need to contain interesting information – the content needs to be excellent – and be presented in an original way.

RSG's Marketing Manager Laura Hope elaborates:

> The findings of research we undertook threw up some negative stereotypes surrounding the recruitment industry, which made the infographic very striking. It gave us scope to show how we can change things. We have shared the infographic widely – with the 5,000 contractors and clients we interviewed and far beyond. People appreciated it because it showed we are really listening to their concerns, and have positive ideas for making things better. It's been widely shared on social media. Overall, we've had a great response.

RSG Resource Solutions Group See: **www.rsg-plc.com/infographic** @rsg-plc

Example of infographic for RSG

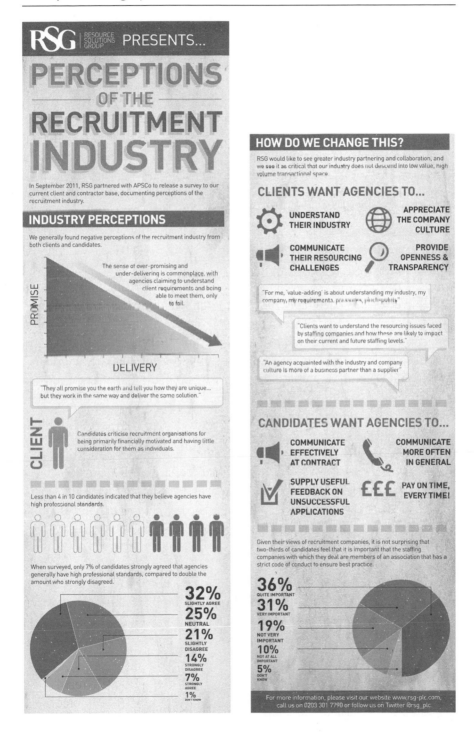

Podcasts for business

Audio can be a powerful medium – and it lets people take your content on the train home.

Bryony Thomas, author of Watertight Marketing **www.bryonythomas.com**
@bryonythomas

Boring commutes, long training runs, quiet lunch breaks are opportunities for people to use their smartphones for entertainment, research or connecting. Aural learners love audio content, so your podcasts could be welcome, if they're valuable. We hope we've stressed the importance of ridding your content of sales messages strongly enough already, but where video or audio is concerned then it's even more crucial. If you're creating content you'd like people to give their valuable downtime to, then it's got to be useful, beautiful or entertaining. A straight sales message just won't cut it. People will turn off.

Podcasts are great for delivering concise information without your users having to download documents, or read through lots of text, and creating one is fairly straightforward. All you need is your computer, a microphone, and a connection to the Internet, and you can get going. There are lots of helpful step-by-step 'how to do it' guides available – try **http://businessandblogs.com/how-to-make-a-podcast**. An MP3 player, or a computer that enables audio is all your clients need to hear your recordings, so you could make one today, and be broadcasting worldwide tomorrow.

Interviews. Hearing a real conversation rather than reading a transcript of it makes ideas come alive. Talking with a client, or colleagues, about a subject you know is of interest to your market makes for a good podcast. If you're the interviewer, keep the talk on track. You know what will be interesting to your listeners so ask questions that steer the conversation back to the really important stuff.

Tips. Not all blog ideas will work as podcasts, but the Valuable Content stalwart of five ways to do this and 10 ways to do that translates well to a podcast. It works for all the same reasons it works as web copy – it's quick, rewarding and feeds the hunger for information now – but it widens your reach to people who'd rather listen and learn, than read.

How-tos. Accessible audio guides that teach people things they really want to know are very valuable content. How to talk to children about divorce; how to win a planning appeal; how to prepare for your first marathon. Whatever line of business you're in, there will be useful nuggets that you can record and share with your audience.

> **Valuable Tip**
>
> Listen to a selection of podcasts produced by people in your field. Which style would your customers find most useful?

Online games as sales tools

Entertainment is one of the key reasons people use the web, so smart companies are creating branded entertaining content to keep their company name in front of clients. Companies that need to give personality to technical products are leading the way. Hewlett Packard is one example. David Nutley of Nutley and Nutley who designs and builds online games for HP explains why:

> It's a great way for companies to show a human face, rather than bombarding clients with constant sales messages. We build a game, something fun and highly competitive – leader boards are good motivators – with a good prize, and invite a targeted list of people to join it. People really enjoy them. You can tell that people are logging on every day, updating their scores, and completing additional tasks for extra points. Online games work far better for some of our clients than straight advertising. You've no way of knowing if your message has been read with a print ad. But with a game, you know that Mr X played the game six times last week. You're definitely on his radar.

http://www.nutleys.com

Mobile apps

Our love affair with our mobile phones has led to an explosion of mobile apps. Want to know the weather? Find your way round Barcelona? Translate your email into Polish? There's an app for it, and over 500,000 others offering informative, entertaining and useful content. Businesses are harnessing this technology to create apps that take their brands straight into the hands of their customers. Is there an app in your business? App Furnace (**www.appfurnace.com**) highlights the following characteristics of successful apps:

- They serve a single purpose. Unlike websites where visitors are happy to explore, app users want to meet their goal in as few taps as possible.

- They provide linear navigation. From top to bottom, like a book page.

- They embrace the technology on offer. GPS, camera, QR codes all make apps more engaging.

- They're tactile. People will hold, tap, stroke, spin, shake an app. The best ones use this to enhance the user's experience.

- Designed for fingers (or thumbs). They're easy to use.

Apps that help your customers are another form of valuable content. Designer Alister Wynn (**www.thisisyoke.com**) agrees:

> More and more of us are using our phones to access services that traditionally would be accessed through the laptop or workstation, so providing a mobile specific version of your service means that you are catering for an ever-increasing percentage of your users.

Valuable Tip

A good app is one that fills a genuine need, is designed well, is accessible and is highly useable.

Lots to choose from. Don't restrict yourself to the written word and you'll find more ways to connect with more people.

Take action

- Research videos and podcasts that have been produced in your sector. Which approach would fit best for your clients and customers?

- Use your network to identify recommended video companies you could work with.

- Would a webinar work in your sector? Test the waters with your network.

CHAPTER 11
WIDEN YOUR REACH:
TAKE YOUR CONTENT
ON TOUR

Content is your champagne and, when used appropriately, PR can pop the cork.

Hubspot www.hubspot.com @hubspot

In this chapter:

- How valuable content wins you PR opportunities.
- Getting your content published in industry-leading media.
- The etiquette of guest blogging.
- Making the most of speaker opportunities.

Follow the advice in the previous chapters and you will build a great foundation for your marketing. All this valuable content will be proving your expertise and sharing knowledge that people are hungry for, drawing leads into your business. Now is the time to really widen your reach and establish your authority in your chosen niche.

This chapter explains how to get your content and ideas in front of a much wider audience for even greater success. You can call this PR (public relations) or simply think of it as taking your content on tour.

How valuable content wins you PR opportunties

If you are regularly sharing valuable content in a variety of formats that really meets the needs of your specific audience you will attract the attention not just of prospects but also of influential people in your field. The connections you build can open new doors for you and widen your marketing scope.

Niche web development firm Newfangled have been asked to speak and write very widely in their industry because of the strength of the content they share:

> Because the content on our website does such a thorough job of documenting our expertise on a continual basis, it has attracted the attention of many prospects, but also other key influencers in our field whom we are able to foster relationships with. These relationships open doors which enable us to start engaging in a wide array of off-site marketing activities such as speaking at key industry events, publishing in industry journals, and publishing books through the right industry publishers. All of those opportunities originated because of the strength of our site.

> Mark O'Brien, president of Newfangled Web Developers **www.newfangled.com** @newfangled_mark

Consultant Mel Lester's content also lands him regular speaker slots:

> My blog has led to really high search engine rankings. This, coupled with producing free e-books and some informal in-person relationships, has led to speaking engagements, which create even more leverage in a wonderful expanding marketing loop.

> Mel Lester **www.bizedge.biz** @mellester

Ascentor's focus on providing valuable content is building their reputation as recognized experts in their field, and recently landed them an opportunity with the BBC:

> Only a couple of months after launching our new content-rich website we were approached by an industry-leading body to post our articles on their site. This was a real coup for us: we have a growing list of followers but they have thousands of readers every day. It gives us far more exposure, boosting our credibility and expanding our reach. The following month we were lucky enough to be featured in an article on information security on the BBC news

website. These opportunities all stemmed from the authoritative nature of the valuable content we share, and business is coming in.

Dave James, MD of information risk management firm Ascentor
www.ascentor.co.uk @ascentor

Whether it's an opportunity on the web, in print, on TV or radio, this kind of free publicity is invaluable. It is an inexpensive way of getting your message out far wider than you can do alone, building awareness, respect and interest in what you do. Search engines will reward you too. If your content is shared on other highly ranked websites it will do wonders for your ranking in search and increase traffic to your site.

Valuable Tip

It is flattering to be asked but with each new opportunity check this is the right forum for you. Does it meet your goals and reach your kind of audience? Use your time judiciously and measure the outcome too.

Getting your content published in industry-leading media

Once you've built up a substantial bank of valuable content on your website, it makes sense to bring it to a wider audience. Hunt for opportunities for writing and publishing articles on other well-respected websites, blogs, journals and publications, and speaker platforms. Do your research and make contact. Most publications and media – onsite and off – are keen for great content.

If your regular content is relevant and of high enough quality and you approach them in the right way, you have a good chance of getting your articles onto their site. Here is how to increase your odds.

- Build relationships with the publishing team or journalists on social media and via their blog if they have one before you contact them.

- Make your approach personal and relevant. Do your research and write for their needs. Don't blanket bomb the same message to multiple sites.

- Don't be pushy or beg.

- Know the site/publication you are writing for very well. Know what topics have already been covered, what tone and style works here.

- If they have writers' guidelines follow them to the letter. If they don't, ask the publisher if they have any guidelines for you. Get the required word-count right, and they'll love you!

- Write stories, not pitches.

- Offer the best post you can; make sure it's relevant; check it carefully for any mistakes and don't use a post that has already been guest-posted elsewhere.

- Once it is accepted (hooray!) be patient. It can take a while to appear on the site. Don't hassle.

My book deal came as a result of posting a series of articles on the Business Zone site – a much visited business site. A Financial Times/Prentice Hall editor found me there, liked my writing and suggested I put forward a proposal.

Heather Townsend, author of the FT Guide to Business Networking

Valuable Tip

Even when you are writing for other websites, all the valuable rules apply. Write articles that are wholly client-focused, and that answer the questions you know people have in your field. Your regular syndicated spot will swiftly vanish if you write sales copy for your own services!

Look for reputable sites, not article directories

We are firm believers in quality over quantity. Blasting the same article to a thousand article directories and link farms is a manipulative technique to boost website authority that is thankfully losing its power thanks to recent search engine algorithm improvements.

Here is Google's take on article marketing on article directory sites:

> *Honestly, I'm not a huge fan of article marketing. Typically the sorts of sites that just republish these articles are not the highest quality sites.*

Google's Head of Web Spam, Matt Culls

Just provide genuinely valuable content on your site and others that your type of buyers find useful. Anything else is a waste of your time.

The etiquette of guest blogging

Posting your articles on other relevant blogs will increase awareness of your own site. It shows you have the respect of your peers – no one is going to share their website space with someone they don't think very highly of. If you share top-notch content and build up relationships via social networking you may well find that other bloggers find you and ask you to write a guest post for their readers. Here's how to play the opportunity.

- Share a clear plan of what you are going to write with your host. They will usually want your perspective on their area of expertise.
- Share really useful information in the post, don't hold back because it's someone else's site.
- Don't promote your own services in the article.
- Do promote the guest blog article widely, referencing your host as you do.
- Return the favour – if your host's blog is relevant to your audience spotlight them on your website.

Making the most of speaker opportunities

Spreading your valuable content wider and raising your profile as an expert in your field can lead naturally to speaking opportunities, or act as useful credentials if you want to actively pursue speaking engagements as a way of expanding your network.

Seven top tips for perfect presentations

1 Remember, it's not all about you. Know your audience and talk about how they can solve their particular challenges.

2 Be clear on the purpose of your talk and build it around a clear central message.

3 If you speak with passion people will find it fascinating. Talk on subjects you care deeply about.

4 Tell stories if you want to be engaging. Unless you are appearing on *Dragon's Den* this is not a platform to pitch your services.

5 Ditch the bulleted PowerPoint slides. Slides are great for sharing images, charts, perhaps quotes, but never read off your slides. Illustrate your points in a creative, colourful way. A short video often works well.

6 Prepare. Don't wing it. Practise, practise, practise.

7 Get a professional to video your speech and post this on your website. This is really valuable content. Share your notes and handouts too.

Presenting is all about relationships. There is a conversation taking place, it's just that you are probably doing most of the talking. But there ought to be engagement and interaction. Make sure you are really contacting and connecting with your audience.

Michael Maynard, Maynard Leigh **www.maynardleigh.co.uk** @maynardleigh

Notice how many of the points above echo the valuable principles in Chapter 3. Spoken or written, remote or face-to-face; valuable communications are the ones that hit home.

Valuable Tip

'Remember that every member of an audience is probably asking themselves three questions about the speaker: Why are they saying this? Why are they saying this – to me? Why are they saying this to me – now?'

Michael Maynard **www.maynardleigh.co.uk** @maynardleigh

Take action

- Which industry websites would you like your blogs to appear on? Connect on Twitter.

- Which bloggers would offer value to your clients and customers? Ask them to guest post for you.

- If you're working on some deeper content, keep your eyes open for speaking opportunities where you could spread the word. Ask your network.

Further reading

The New Rules of Marketing & PR: How to use news releases, blogs, podcasting, viral marketing & online media to reach buyers directly, 3rd edn, David Meerman Scott, Wiley, 2011

Perfect Presentations, Andrew Leigh and Michael Maynard, Random House Books, 2009

CHAPTER 12
VALUABLE CONTENT
FOR SALESPEOPLE

You can't stay in your corner of the forest waiting for others to come to you. You have to go to them sometimes.

Winnie the Pooh

In this chapter:

- How to use content to start sales conversations.
- Valuable content, not brochures.
- Tips for valuable content sales campaigns.
- The art of good sales copy.
- Valuable content and the power of good sales follow-up.
- Bringing sales and marketing closer together.

This chapter is for salespeople. It shows you how to use valuable content proactively to help you win more business.

If your company follows the marketing advice in this book it will draw leads into the business for you to convert into sales. All this valuable content spreading around the web will bring you a satisfying increase in inbound leads. People will find you via your website, your blogs and deeper content, and your growing social networks. They will learn to trust you and remember you through the value of the information you deliver. Creating and sharing valuable content is an excellent 'pull' or 'inbound' marketing strategy and, executed in the right way, it is a highly effective 'push' or 'outbound' sales approach too.

As we mentioned way back in the first chapter, many outbound lead-generation techniques such as traditional direct mail campaigns and telemarketing are not working as well as they used to. If you are in a sales role this is tough. You are measured and rewarded on the revenue you generate for the business. If tried and tested techniques don't work then how do you justify your position and find new clients?

This chapter will show you how to create and use valuable content to help you open doors and make direct contact with people who have never heard of you before – the hardest job for any salesperson. It will show you how to use valuable content as a 'push' strategy that won't switch off potential new clients. Get it right and selling will hit the mark with your prospects and customers. Here's how to do it.

How to use content to start sales conversations

Valuable content is the perfect conversation starter for people you want to do business with. It flies under an organization's anti-marketing radar, because it is useful. Lead with the valuable stuff – send an article, an e-book or even a printed book – and you will earn the right to engage with prospects.

> *Well-researched and valuable content demonstrates better than anything else that you understand your buyer's world and most importantly their critical success factors, then the buyers will find you more interesting and will be much more willing to meet you.*
>
> David Tovey, author of *Principled Selling* **www.principledselling.org** @principledsell

If the prospect you want to meet feels there is already a relationship based on your marketing activities they will be more motivated to meet you and spend time with you to explore opportunities to do business together. You will have a better, warmer sales meeting.

The key, as ever, is to start by knowing who you want to work for (we like the 'dream clients' phrase David Tovey uses in the *Principled Selling* book mentioned above). Be crystal clear on their needs and interests and provide content that hits that sweetspot. Continue to deliver value with each and every contact.

> **Valuable Tip**
>
> Remember that the prospects you are targeting are as busy, as cynical, as suspicious and over-sold to as you. The only way to stop people hitting the delete button or marking your email as spam is to provide something that they find interesting and of value.

Valuable content, not brochures

Stop spending money on brochures and invest in creating valuable content for your sales team instead. Brochures do not engage. They are only useful when the hardest part of marketing has been done – a quick credibility booster further down the line, not an engagement tool.

Bryony Thomas, author of *Watertight Marketing* **www.bryonythomas.com** @bryonythomas

If you are looking to engage prospects and get sales meetings focus your marketing budget on creating valuable content rather than producing costly brochures and sales presentations. Brochures are still useful, but for a professional firm they are purely a credibility tool not a door opener. Here is a story of a forward-thinking company that sends valuable content not brochures for sales success.

Conscious Solutions' sales team lead with valuable content

David Gilroy, Sales and Marketing Director of Conscious Solutions, a specialist provider of digital marketing services for UK law firms, is a great believer in valuable content to engage prospects and initiate sales. Theirs is a niche proposition for the top 4,500 out of 11,000 law firms in the UK and they know their market well. Conscious' content-rich website and social media activity generates leads and referrals but with ambitious growth plans they want more to meet their goals. They take their content to their market and this strategy gets them sales results.

David and his sales team don't produce any brochures. Instead they have created a stack of useful, well-designed guides for law firms held as downloadable e-books in PDF format on their site and in printed format too – guides such as *38 Common Mistakes Law Firms Still Make with their Websites*, *29 Mistakes Law Firms Unwittingly Make with their Brand*.

Our valuable guides – in e-book and printed format – are the only marketing materials my sales team needs. Guides, not brochures, open new doors and get us good meetings and sales.

David Gilroy, Director of Conscious Solutions @conscioussol

They conduct *valuable content campaigns* around each guide, sending carefully written emails to target contacts with a link to download the guide from the Conscious website. Each campaign builds their reputation as helpful experts in their field and generates around a 15 per cent response rate. If someone clicks the download button then Conscious' website alerts the team and a salesperson will call '... to see if the booklet downloaded OK'. It's a perfect conversation starter rather than a 'hard sell' conversation.

As well as the email campaign David's team advertises the guide with pay-per-click LinkedIn adverts. David tracks the result of each campaign carefully to monitor return on investment and to learn what works best. In August to September 2011 Conscious ran a LinkedIn ad campaign targeted at people whose LinkedIn profile said they worked in the legal sector. The total spend was £3,636. Conscious' average ROI target for this spend was £28,800. The campaign was promoting one of their valuable content tips booklets – 1,214 click throughs generated 104 downloads; 50 effective conversations generated 12 sales opportunities, which resulted in £35,050 of sales with an outstanding pipeline (as of April 2012) of £22,280. A successful campaign by any measure, and the valuable content was a key part.

See **www.conscious.co.uk**

Valuable Tip

If you invest in advertising, whether this is Google Adwords, or LinkedIn advertising like Conscious Solutions, you'll get better results by promoting your valuable content rather than your services.

Tips for valuable content sales campaigns

If you want to meet with a dream prospect build a personal valuable content marketing campaign just for them. It might be based on two or three emails or tailored letters sent over several weeks with a different, interesting and useful article attached. Valuable content campaigns are highly effective in getting meetings with key people and in helping to build a trusted relationship.

20 tips for a successful valuable content campaign:

1 Know exactly who you want to do business with – do your research.

2 Create something they'll find useful, relevant and interesting – an e-book for example.

3 Have your sales team send this e-book to your dream prospects.

4 Craft the introductory email or letter carefully – help, don't pitch.

5 Put the e-book on your website.

6 Create a great landing page for it on your site.

7 Promote the e-book on your home page.

8 Make sure the e-book content is optimized for search.

9 Blog about it.

10 Tweet about it.

11 Share it as a LinkedIn status update.

12 Mention it on your LinkedIn groups, if it's relevant.

13 Turn it into a slideshow.

14 Feature it in your email newsletter.

15 Advertise it with a targeted pay-per-click display ad – LinkedIn is particularly good for professional firms.

16 Put a link to it on your email signature.

17 Put a link to it on the back of a business card.

18 Create a webinar on the subject and invite your network to attend.

19 Create and distribute a press release about it.

20 Track the results carefully, and create a case study to show top management the benefits that your valuable content strategy is delivering.

The art of good sales copy

Getting your initial communication right is absolutely crucial. It's all in the approach. Whether it is by email or post, when you are communicating with someone you have never met before the sentiment should be:

We understand your world. You are the kind of person we'd love to do business with. To prove it, here's something really useful/fascinating. We've helped other good businesses just like you to get fantastic results. Call me if you'd like to talk this through.

Successful sales approaches are personal, interesting and respectful and give the receiver choice.

Good copy, bad copy by Matthew Curry

Matthew Curry, Head of E Commerce at Lovehoney (**www.lovehoney.com**) receives a lot of cold sales emails from hopeful suppliers keen to do business with him. Here are a couple of different types of sales emails he's been sent, with his comments on what works and what leaves him cold.

A. How not to write sales copy

Email subject line: ARE YOU NOT DEGRUMPETIZING™ YOUR CUSTOMERS???!

Matthew, I'd just like to introduce Silver Telephone to you. We're a dynamic 360 full service turnkey solutions provider, helping you to fully degrumpetize™ your full lifecycle revenue stream through innovative synergies of viral and crowd source campaigning. We've degrumpetized™ for Best Buy, Walgreens and Alabama Mama Maternitywear.

Matthew, can you give me a good time for a 15-minute call about how Love Honey can take control of your degrumpetization™ strategy?

John E Carson

Silver Telephone LLC

Alabama

Why this sales copy doesn't work

1 Endless ™ symbols everywhere. If you're trying to sell me something ™'d, I'm going to immediately think 'they've taken a well-known concept, that I probably already do, branded it, and are trying to sell it as a service'. In this case, Degrumpetizing just means complaint management.

2 Unnecessary words to look impressive. Turnkey means 'we do stuff'; full-service means 'we'll try to do everything to get more money from you whether we're good at it or not'; 'innovative' rarely is, and using 'synergies' and 'viral' is a sure-fire way of making me press the spam button.

3   Which is a good point; nowadays, the spam button is so close to the delete button, you're lucky if you only get deleted.

4   Having references in a different country, and businesses nothing like mine. If you think you can help, show me you've done it for a company similar to mine (but not a direct competitor, that would really annoy me).

5   Starting paragraphs with my first name gets my back up. Too personal, too fast.

6   Getting the name of my company wrong is ridiculous. Either you've bought my details from an old list, or you're just too lazy to check.

7   Having an American address, when you're approaching a British company.

B. A better, more valuable sales approach

Email subject line: Does Lovehoney have a problem with customer complaints?

Hello Mr Curry. If you're not sure about how well Lovehoney handles customer complaints, we can help.

Visit our site for a 5-step method of working out your complaint handling success rate. This is a great consistent metric that you can measure each month to see how well you're doing.

If your success rate is less than 90%, we think that Lovehoney could be even better by tackling customer complaints in a different way.

Silver Telephone makes software, and consults, on improving customer complaint handling. We're really good at it, and it's not just us who says so, we've worked with Firebox, Boots and Agent Provocateur. We'll happily pass on their details if you'd like to speak to them about us.

Work out your handling success rate, and if you think you need us, get in touch. Hopefully we won't hear from you!

Kind regards

Alison,

Alison Tabbernacle,

Silver Telephone

Why this sales approach works

1   It has an enticing headline.

2   It doesn't presume I have a problem.

3   It shows me how I can find out if I have a problem – it's useful.

4   It gives me a criteria where I should consider help.

5   It tells me exactly what the company does.

6   It gives me UK companies, with similar business models and customers to mine.

7 It offers proof in terms of references.

8 It's funny, with the sign off that they hope they don't hear from me.

Notice that the valuable sales copy is short, to the point, and shows it understands the recipient's world in a simple sentence. It works because it was sent to exactly the right person – and that's the key. Had your Mum received it, it might have felt like spam, but it was well-targeted and relevant.

> ## Valuable Tip
>
> If you want to stand apart, think about sending letters by good old-fashioned post.

Don't discount direct mail. In these days where we're overwhelmed with email, good old direct mail is making a comeback. Not flyers and adverts – but well-written letters that offer something of value rather than a sales pitch. And hand addressed. Even better: send 'lumpy mail' – a package with a relevant object accompanying the letter. Who doesn't open packages?

Ian Brodie, More Clients Blog **www.ianbrodie.com** @ianbrodie

Quick checklist for valuable sales emails and letters:

- addressed to the right person;
- compelling headline;
- engaging;
- empathizes with the reader;
- clear offer;
- easy to read;
- nicely designed;
- humble;
- useful, not hard sell;
- credible;
- jargon-free;
- interesting;

- short and to-the-point;
- links to find out more.

> **Valuable Tip**
>
> If you struggle to write compelling sales communication hire a good
> sales copywriter to help you.

Valuable content and the power of good sales follow-up

Not everyone will buy at the first sales meeting. Inertia, lack of time, other
more pressing matters to deal with, budget constraints – there are many valid
reasons why the first sales meeting does not immediately lead to a sale. Yet
according to research only 20 per cent of sales leads are ever followed up.
That's a shining pile of sales opportunity lost without a trace, simply due to
lack of good follow-up.

Valuable content makes for perfect sales follow-up. Instead of strong-arm
closing or increasingly desperate demands for a decision, keep the dialogue
open by sending your prospect information that they will value – the *saw this
and thought of you* strategy:

- Send a link to industry news and research that proves the urgency of
  the approach you recommended.
- Write an article that reminds them of the benefits of your solution and
  nudges them towards the sale.
- Invite them to join your mailing list and send valuable newsletters and
  updates to build trust and keep you front of mind until they are ready
  to buy.

Valuable content is highly effective when used at the proposal/presentation
stage and to keep in touch after putting in a proposal without seeming pushy.
The content has to stay relevant. If the client feels that they have been put on
a database and sent a generic email you will lose their credibility and enthusiasm.
Be valuable, stay relevant.

Bringing sales and marketing closer together

If you are in sales you are in the perfect position to come up with ideas for valuable content. You hear first-hand the questions that prospects and customers ask about your industry, your products or services. Ask marketing to help you create valuable collateral that answers these questions – FAQs on your website, articles on your blog, case studies in written or video format written from the customer point of view, a white paper or e-book that solves a pertinent problem. This is just the kind of collateral that will get you the sales results you need. Both marketing and salespeople at the coalface of customer communication have a role to play here. Creating valuable content is a great opportunity to get the two departments working closer together.

Valuable content eases the sales process at every step. Use it to help you open doors, nurture those leads and close sales and you will build stronger relationships with clients and customers.

Take action

- Idenitify the content you already have in your business. Is it valuable enough to send to potential clients?

- Use your knowledge of the people you're targeting. Plan three pieces of content you'd be happy to use to open doors.

- Write an article or get the marketing team in your business to help you create the e-book, video, download or white paper you need to kick-start more conversations.

Further reading

Principled Selling: How to win more business without selling your soul, David Tovey, Kogan Page, 2012

Trust-based Selling: Using customer focus and collaboration to build long-term relationships, Charles H Green, McGraw Hill, 2006

The Trusted Advisor, David H Maister, Charles H Green, and Robert M Galford, Simon & Schuster, 2002

PART THREE

HOW TO MAKE YOUR
MARKETING VALUABLE?

Valuable Content Marketing In Action

OUR IDEAS

customer NEEDS

* GOALS *

X Y Z

* CONTENT CALENDAR *

JAN MAR MAY

- 3 BLOGS ON **Y**
- 1 VIDEO ON **X**
- 1 DOWNLOAD ON **Z**

- 4 BLOGS ON **X+Y**
- 1 CASE STUDY ON **Y**
- 1 PODCAST ON **Z**

- 1 VIDEO ON **Z**
- 5 BLOGS ON **X**
- 1 NEWSLETTER ON **Y**

* ME! * I'll take that! THE TEAM * ALREADY ON THE CASE... * DONE!

CHAPTER 13
HOW TO WRITE CONTENT YOUR CUSTOMERS WILL VALUE

When asked, 'How do you write?'
I invariably answer, one word at a time.

Stephen King, author

In this chapter:

- Making your writing valuable.
- How to be engaging.
- How to write less and say more.
- Help with headlines.
- Making time for writing.
- Break it down – making writing manageable.
- The importance of editing.
- How to stop procrastinating and just do it!

So, you know why you need to produce first class content to market your business, and you've got a list of things you're going to write.

The act of writing itself can feel like a huge hurdle – many people feel they just can't do it, or can't do it well enough to make it the main focus of their business marketing. This chapter will help you with some of the less tangible aspects of writing – how to get your tone of voice right and how to be engaging. Not just how to write, but how to produce writing that people will value. There is some practical advice on getting it done – making time for writing, making the task manageable, and just plain getting on and doing it!

Our advice is to give it a go; like any skill, writing improves with lots of practice. We guarantee the act of writing blogs will improve your understanding of your field, and your connection with your customers and clients. Writing is thinking, really valuable thinking, and doing it will help you build a stronger business.

If you do decide you'd be happier employing a copywriter to help you create your content, then use this chapter to help you recognize the qualities you need to look for in the content you outsource, and to frame your discussions with a copywriter.

Make your writing valuable

The key things to think about with any piece of writing, whether it's an e-book, a blog, a web page or a Tweet, are:

- your audience (who's reading it);
- the subject (what you're writing about);
- your tone of voice (how you're saying it).

Know your audience

Understanding your clients and customers inside out is what drives the content you produce.

Development Done Right writes the right stuff

Development Done Right is a web development company that specializes in helping creative agencies. The work they do is so technical that it lives in a deep, dark techy subculture, not visited by people in daylight, out of black T-shirts. Development Done Right's clients need their expertise, but they don't talk or think in a technical way themselves. From their point of view, they just need stuff to happen to make their projects happen.

Because of this, Development Done Right doesn't communicate with its audience about coding. It talks about functionality and the business impact of having a state-of-the-art website. The kind of blog articles they write are designed to be useful to someone working in a creative agency – they give them an appropriate level of knowledge to be able to do their jobs better. They don't need a complicated analysis of Java coding; however, something that puts them in a better position next time they are working on a web design pitch is really useful.

See **www.developmentdoneright.co.uk**

Valuable Tip

Think of a real client when you're composing your content; it will make your writing warmer and easier to connect with. Try our 'Get to know your customers' template in the Resources section.

Pick the right subject

To appeal to their technologically demanding, but technically inexperienced audience, the Development Done Right team blog about web development from an agency's point of view. They pick subjects that frame their knowledge in an accessible and useful way:

- Ten things you need to know about e-commerce but were afraid to ask.
- Five things to ask at the start of a web development project.
- What your clients need to understand about content management systems.

Knowledge isn't everything; it's what you do with it that counts. There may be equally technically astute web developers out there, but what agencies need are web developers that understand the challenges they are facing, and help them navigate them successfully.

> **Valuable Tip**
>
> Only pick subjects your audience cares about.

Tone of voice

Tone of voice can be a difficult thing to get right when you first start writing. The danger is you sound stilted, or unnatural. The fear that you might get it wrong, or come across as unintelligent, makes some people write in an artificially proper and convoluted way. This up-tightness doesn't translate into good content.

For example, don't say 'we facilitate training sessions to leverage optimal grassroots success', say 'we run coaching workshops for new businesses'.

What you're aiming for in any blog, Tweet or web page is connection. Don't let awkward language or unnecessary jargon get in the way.

There's no generic tone of voice that suits every business. How a web design agency speaks is not the same as a firm of solicitors; an HR firm sounds different from a chain of Italian restaurants. Good content shares similarities – it's clear, concise and easily understood – but the variances in tone of voice are important for building your business brand. So how do you get the tone of voice right for your business?

Start with speaking, not writing. How would you talk to a client that you're working with? What words would you use to explain what you mean if they were sitting right next to you? Chances are you'd want to make it as easy as possible for them to follow. Expertise can be a stumbling block if you just dump it in somebody's path, so see what you're saying from their point of view.

Talking first can establish the right lexicon of words for you to draw from. It should eliminate all but the most clearly understood jargon in your sector – the terms that everyone uses and understands completely – the words your clients would expect to see as part of their working lives. You wouldn't throw in something your client wouldn't understand if you were chatting through a project over a coffee – blank faces are disconcerting and don't make for comfortable meetings – so don't put them into your articles and blogs.

Break it up a bit. Vary sentence length for interest and readability. It might help to record yourself speaking to begin with. Mimicking your natural speech patterns can be a good place to start, and it helps break you away from writing in a flat way. When we speak we vary our sentence structure. Sometimes we speak in very long sentences that meander and wind around and come back to the beginning again. Other times we don't. Getting some of this variety into your writing helps establish an authentic and natural-sounding tone of voice. Again, you're aiming for connection – and keeping your reader interested in what you've got to say is part of staying connected.

Valuable Tip

Sharon uses Dragon Dictate, a free iPhone app to help with first drafts of blog articles.

How to be engaging

Always try to envisage things from the reader's point of view. What are they thinking and feeling? What's bothering them and what do they want to hear? How can I draw them in and keep them reading?

Jim O'Connor, *Stories that Sell* **www.storiesthatsell.co.uk** @whitecottage1

Whether you're writing as Head of Chambers, or as the owner of a recruitment agency, you want to engage with your reader. You'd like them to stay with you for the length of the article, at the very least, and to have gained something of value by the end of it.

Being engaging is about being likeable and interesting. It's mostly to do with demonstrating you genuinely understand your client's perspective, and showing some personality. Being a real person, not a job title, makes you easier to connect with. Think of the articles you enjoy reading – the best ones give a sense of the writer as well as the subject. It's their opinion or take on a subject, rather than the subject itself, that keeps your interest.

Analogies are a really good way to be engaging and make connections with your readers. Making comparisons can throw up some fantastically memorable phrases that make points quickly and strongly. For example, if I'm trying to explain how a website home page shouldn't look, I could say 'Disorganized, chaotic, cheap, scruffy, a bit all over the place, full of tarnished sales messages, don't know where to look, invokes an overwhelming feeling of 'Oh I can't be bothered'. Or I could say 'Like the sales floor of a department store after the first day of the January Sales.' The analogy says it far faster, and gives the reader an image they can quickly grasp and will be able to recall.

Be yourself. Get up close and personal. (But not too personal.) Throwing in some real-life details into your blogging will keep people reading, but make sure it's for the right reason. For example, if you were writing about times in business when things haven't gone so well, it's fine to mention the feelings it brought back about when you failed your driving test when you were 19, but avoid anything too close to the bone. You want to write in a friendly, easy style which is comfortable for the reader. By all means relate personal stories around commonplace things – buying a car, renovating a house, raising kids – but don't give away anything that is truly private and personal in your life.

Use an active voice. An engaging tone of voice is rarely passive. Look at the way writers that motivate you use words, and you'll almost certainly find they use an active voice. Your choice of words can put you in control or shuffle you onto the sidelines. Using an active voice gives your words authority too. Don't say 'the report will be delivered', say 'we'll deliver the report'. It's much more powerful.

Another trick good content writers use to get some energy into their copy is to focus on the beginnings of sentences. Look at the first words in each of your lines and make sure they're different. Long lines of we do this and we do that are dull. Yawn, yawn. Throw in some new ones.

How to write less and say more

The best business writing is direct, and like all good writing, makes a connection with its reader.

People read differently on websites so you'll have to write differently too. Speed is the biggest difference; we don't give anything on a website the same time as we would if we were holding it in our hands. Web pages are scanned, rather than read like a book, so you need to make sure your web content makes sense to the speed scanner.

Valuable Tip

When writing for the web you need to write in an inverted pyramid style of writing, which means starting with your most important point first. Aim for half the word count for an article written for the web, than one written for print.

- **Be very clear about the purpose of each section.** Knowing exactly what your readers want to find makes it easier to start shaping the content.

- **Don't try to make too many points on each page.** Focus on getting one message across strongly, rather than showering the page with weaker points. (You can always add more pages. An engaged reader will be eager to explore further, and drip feeding works better than a huge wall of text.)

- **Work on your sentence structure.** Rid your lines of slow-you-down conjunctives. So no 'however's, or 'moreover's, or 'hereby's.

- **Using active verbs** in the present tense gives the impression of purpose – just what you want to make readers feel they're getting somewhere fast.

- **Short sentences make for an easy read.**

- **Metaphors** condense ideas and feelings succinctly, so weave some in and cut straight to the heart. Pick ones with an emotional resonance to pull readers in and make them more receptive to your message.

- **Can the cans.** Don't say 'we can deliver x', say 'we deliver x'.

- **White space helps your readers breathe.** Overloaded webpages make readers feel like they're stuck in a tube train during rush hour. You might be telling them something interesting, but all they can think about is getting out.

- **Make it scannable.** Use headlines as scaffolding to sum up your main points and give your content structure. Signposting with headlines is a great way to make web pages fast, rewarding reads.

- **Finally, embrace editing.** Write it, leave it, come back with new eyes and cut out anything that isn't absolutely necessary.

Help with headlines

On average, five times as many people read the headlines as read the body copy so learning to write good headlines is a valuable writing skill to master. Faced with an immense sea of information, we scan for headlines that pull us in and anchor us to something relevant. Headlines matter on web pages, and even more so on social media sites like Twitter. Here's how to get people to click on yours instead of swimming past:

- **Be succinct.** Summarize the point of your article or blog in as few words as possible. Short and snappy is more appealing than convoluted. It's a good test of your content too – if you can't sum up the point in a sentence, maybe you haven't got it quite right yet.

- **Use the keyword on the title.** This is useful for SEO, and potential readers.

- **Put your reader first.** Think about what they want to know. What will they be searching for? How is your content going to help them? Use the phrase they'll be searching for as your headline. Home page design – a quick guide. Networking etiquette – what to say first. Key components of winning press releases. These are examples of reader-focused headlines.

- **Ask a question.** Headlines that engage are good news, and conversational questioning-style headlines do just that. Are your business cards working? Is your recruitment process up to scratch? Do your clients know how to find you?

- **'How to' headlines.** People are searching for information, and the 'How to' headline attracts readers to click for more detail. How to design your About Us page. How to boost e-commerce sales. How to sell your house in six weeks.

- **Promise success.** We all want to succeed, and are tempted by people that offer it to us. Spiking your headlines with positive success words can encourage clicks. Win more clients with smart business networking. Successful sales start with three words. Boost profits with smarter working.

- **Raise the spectre of failure.** Fear of failure is as big a drive as the desire for success. Scare people into reading your stuff! Five costly PR mistakes to avoid. How to lose customers and alienate people. Is your web copy costing you sales?

- **Offer some inside knowledge.** Who doesn't want to know a secret? It's not hard to pique our curiosity. The secrets of successful bloggers. The trait top novelists share. Which blogger do 20 world leaders follow?

- **Play the numbers game.** Maybe it's the promise of a quick read, perhaps because it seems to offer something easily graspable and definitive. Whatever the reason, Twitter can't get enough of the numbers headlines. Five ways to improve your SEO instantly. Seven ways to keep readers on your site. Three writing rules you must break.

- **Get active.** Words like boost, drive, run, leap, soar, make headlines more compelling than passive words. Injecting some energy into your headlines grabs attention. Boost sales with clever marketing. Drive customers to checkout faster.

- **Say something different.** Originality is like a breath of fresh air in the crowded Twitter marketplace. Headlines created from a different lexicon leap off the page. I'm not talking jargon, just unexpected words – nouns or verbs – that shake up the stream of salesy Tweets. What Lady Gaga can teach you about networking. Why Puffins rock at closing the sale.

- **And if all else fails... Capitalize Everything.** It's in your face, brash, and hard to avoid. Personally, I don't like this headline style, but it doesn't stop me clicking if the content is promising. How To Win More Sales Overnight. Why Your Content Sucks. How To Write Killer Blogs.

Making time for writing

Bryony Thomas, author of *Watertight Marketing*, puts aside half a day a week for content creation, plus 10 to 20 minutes a day for social media. She's a regular blogger, and her site also includes videos, guides and other useful downloads. Half a day a week is a good realistic figure to aim for – it will give you enough hours to create worthwhile content, and still have time to do your regular work.

Remember that half a day a week spent on creating valuable content will be time well spent – saving you time on ineffective forms of marketing and building a stronger and more robust business. Because of the results valuable content will generate, this will be your most productive half of a day of each week. Squeezing another task into your week might feel like a struggle, but it is doable. We've mentioned keeping a notebook for blog ideas, and that's one of the best things you can do to make time. A lot of the thinking around your writing happens away from the screen. Jotting down the kernel of an idea and getting on with other stuff lets the ideas percolate away in the back of your mind. When you sit down to actually write you'll find the words come more quickly.

Setting aside time, and guarding it, is important. Find a time that works best for you. Sharon writes better in the mornings, Sonja prefers the evenings. Carve out some time when you'll be at your sharpest, and focus on your writing.

Give yourself deadlines. Seeing your writing as part of your bigger marketing picture should motivate you to finish this article, and start thinking about the next. Making it part of your everyday working routine will ensure you get it done.

Making writing manageable

If writing a 400-word blog feels like a slog, then divide it into chunks and tackle it bit by bit. Even if you find writing easy, it's a good idea to break articles down in this way. Web visitors like reading in sections, so plan your writing in that format:

- 100 words for an introduction setting out the question you're answering.
- 50 words to introduce a list.
- 200 words in list form.
- 50 words summing up.

Different articles will need different weightings of words, but planning how much you will write in each section before you start will save you time, and keep your writing on target.

> ### Valuable Tip
> Use the word count to keep you on target – your software programme will have a word count tool.

The importance of editing

Once you've got into the swing of writing, you'll come to recognize the euphoria that accompanies the finishing of a great blog article. There will be five minutes when what you've just written is the most important thing that's ever been written in the entire world on that subject. There's not a moment to waste – you have to share it now, this very second, your life and the sanity of the world depends upon it!

There's also a drive to be finished with it. Ticking it off your things-to-do list would make you feel better, so you're itching to upload.

The very best thing to do now is not to press send, but to save the document, close it, and go back and look at it again tomorrow with clearer, more cynical eyes.

Just a few hours' distance should make you better able to check the piece for the following common mistakes.

Stop, look, edit – five things to do before you press 'publish':

1 Is it on target? It felt like it was at the time, but writing can be deceptive sometimes. Ask yourself if it is genuinely useful for your clients? It might be that some simple tweaking is all that's needed to pull it back in line, or it might be that you need to put it on hold for longer. Great ideas are never wasted, but they do need the right format to fly. Don't be scared of pulling something if you know it's not right.

2 Have you missed any words out? Easily done when the prose is flying. Check your copy slowly and carefully to make sure it makes sense.

3 Have you repeated words? Again, it's a common mistake when you're writing fast. Check again.

4 Is it spelt right? Is it the right word? Spellcheck picks up most errors – but it won't pick up mis-substituted words. Don't let something go out until it makes perfect sense.

5 Is the grammar right? Developing a natural and engaging tone of voice doesn't mean you can stop writing proper, like. Inaccurate grammar stops readers in their tracks, and it makes your writing hard to understand. If you're not sure, ask someone else to check too. Even if you are sure, a second pair of eyes is never a bad idea.

And finally...

How to stop procrastinating and just do it!

We do know that getting down to doing writing is difficult if you're running your own business. Most of us don't have the luxury of dropping everything and getting away from it all to focus on writing alone. And even when we do get the time, suddenly other things seem more pressing. Should I check my email? Tidy my desk? Have a cup of coffee?

Here are some things that help get writing done:

1 **Remember why you are doing it.**

   The words you are writing are part of your big marketing plan. A small step in the right direction, not a huge hurdle. Get it into proportion.

2 **Don't waste energy thinking about it. Redirect energy into doing it.**

   Just get on with it. Open your computer, don't turn on Twitter, don't look at Facebook, don't open email, just start writing.

3 **The sooner you start the sooner you finish.**

   Anticipate the end. Once you've done it, it's done, and it won't have to be done again. Get on with it!

4 **Promise yourself a treat.**

   It works for small children and for grown ups too – 400 words and I can go for a walk/have a cake/make that phone call.

5 **Carve out some real time, and protect it from other demands.**

   Five minutes a day to record your ideas in a blog diary, half an hour to plan a blog (and write one too, once you're really up and running), an hour and a half to write something that addresses the question that keeps coming up, and get it up on your website.

6 **Remove yourself.**

   Write somewhere different, away from the distractions of your usual working day. A quiet meeting room, a café, a library, even a different desk.

7 **Make a commitment.**

   Deadlines work (it's the only way we ever get our writing done!).

Writing really will make all the difference to your business, so set aside the time, and keep to it.

Take action

- Write a draft of a two-page article titled *'The Top Three Reasons Why...'* and time yourself. Sleep on it.

- Revisit it tomorrow against the checklist and make improvements. Time yourself.

- The following day, write *'The Biggest Benefit Our Customers Get From... is...'* Set a timer for half the time it took to write the first one. Your ultimate aim, through practice, it to be able to write up to two pages within one hour.

Further reading

On Writing, a memoir of the craft, Stephen King, Scribner, 2000

You will find web writing inspiration on www.copyblogger.com and on our website www.valuablecontent.co.uk

CHAPTER 14
MAKING IT HAPPEN:
SEVEN STEPS TO SUCCESS

> *Vision without action is a daydream;*
> *action without vision is a nightmare.*

Japanese proverb

In this chapter:

- Seven steps to success with valuable content.
- How to get clear on what you will talk about.
- Two successful starting strategies to choose from.
- Planning like a pro with a publishing calendar.
- Putting the right team together.
- The need to measure, learn, refine and continue.

How do you transform a business that has only ever promoted itself the traditional way to one that markets itself effectively with valuable content? It is a big change for many and, as you can see from the previous chapters, you have a variety of tools at your disposal, so where do you start?

In this final chapter we give you a simple roadmap to follow for success with your valuable content marketing strategy.

You will find questions and examples to help you along the way. Templates for each stage are available in the Resources section at the back of the book and on our website.

Seven steps to success with valuable content

Seven steps to content success:

1 Know your business objectives.

2 Be clear on what you will talk about.

3 Pick the right mix of content creation and distribution tools.

4 Make sure your website is up to the job.

5 Plan like a publishing pro with a content calendar.

6 Put the right team together.

7 Measure, refine, learn and continue.

Step 1 Know your business objectives

A change makes things different. There must be a From and a To.

Jane Northcote, author of *Making Change Happen* **www.janenorthcote.com**

As with any change, the first step is to know what you are trying to achieve through this new approach to marketing before you get started. Be clear on where your business stands now, and define where you would like it to be. What is the difference you are looking to make by marketing with valuable content?

We will look at some simple, effective measures and measurement tools to help you chart your progress in Step 7 (see page 205). For now, think what you want your new focus on valuable content marketing to achieve for your business. Write it down.

What are you trying to achieve?

- Greater awareness of our firm
- More engagement
- More inbound leads from the web
- Better quality sales leads

- More referrals
- More PR opportunities
- More recruits
- Happier customers
- Happier staff
- BETTER BUSINESS

Step 2 Be clear on what you will talk about

If you are going to create valuable content you need to have something to say. As we discussed in Chapter 3, that something has to be relevant to your business (for it is sales you are after at the end of the day) and meaningful to your clients or customers.

Begin by doing some thinking and research to get clarity on your company's offer and the customer niche(s) you serve. Identify profitable groups in your target market that share common needs, interests and concerns. For some small, focused firms there may be only one group but often it is more.

For each group we suggest you draw up a detailed customer profile or 'buyer persona' as it has become known. This will give you a very clear picture of the types of customer you serve and help you to frame the messages and content you create in their terms.

> *Clear your mind of all the sales blurb, features and benefits surrounding your products and services. Now draft 'buyer personas': archetypes of each distinct, profitable, ideal buyer type in your market. This will keep you on-message when it comes to producing content your prospects find and act on.*
>
> Mick Dickinson, Buzzed Up **www.buzzedup.co.uk** @mickdickinson

To complete your buyer personas research the needs of each target group carefully. Find out what you can and then interview real clients and potential customers in these groups to hear the story in their words. Asking your clients for feedback is hugely powerful. It stops you making up marketing messages in a vacuum, so take the time to listen. Ask about their challenges and goals and the problems you can solve for them. Then you can use their words, not your own.

Who are you talking to and what will you say?

Your service	Your target groups	What questions are they asking	What answers can you provide?
Web design for professional service firms	Senior partners	Will a new website really bring business benefit?	Case study: How a new website improved our bottom line
Web design for professional services firms	Business managers	How do we find the right agency to build our website?	Checklist: Essential questions to ask a professional services web design agency
Web design for professional services firms	Marketing managers	How will a new website raise our profile?	Blog: 20 ways marketing with valuable content gets people talking

Basing your work on buyer personas prevents you from sitting on your butt in your comfortable office just making stuff up, which is the cause of most ineffective marketing.

David Meerman Scott, author of The New Rules of Marketing and PR
www.webinknow.com @dmscott

Use all this research to paint a clear picture of the people you want to do business with and the content they will value most.

Taking the web design professional service firms example in the table above, here are a couple of different personas to show you what we mean.

Two buyer personas

Persona 1: The senior partner

James (50) is a partner in a medium-sized law firm (50 employees). The changing legal market is a big concern for him, and he understands very clearly the threat that Tesco etc pose to firms of his size. Staff cuts are on the cards, and he feels uneasy about spending more money on marketing with no proven ROI when belts are being tightened elsewhere. He doesn't use social media either for work or at home – (his teenage children tell him he should try Facebook and Twitter) but his laptop home page is set to BBC Business News. He trusts them to keep him updated.

James' goals

To ride out the coming storm and secure his firm's position. He has a real belief in the quality of the service his firm provides, and wishes there was a way of communicating that, without risking limited funds. To feel secure.

Content ideas for James:

1   White paper on ROI on website spend in professional services sector.

2   Video case study of law firm that invested in website and social media. Firm of similar size and client base.

3   Article by respected commentator on changing client trust behaviour and web marketing for professional firms.

Persona 2: The marketing manager

Sarah (41) is the new marketing manager for a large firm of accountants. She knows her marketing stuff, and is keen to get the partners blogging and Tweeting but her efforts are being met with internal resistance. No one has the time, and to be honest, they don't really see the point. Her initial enthusiasm for her role is being worn down. She knows what the firm should do, but is wearily pessimistic of the chances of making that happen. She is putting tentative feelers out for new marketing positions.

Sarah's goals

To prove her worth, to make a success of this new role, and to see her marketing ideas making a difference.

Content ideas for Sarah:

1   E-book on why accountants need to blog – and how to make them do it.

2   Article: 'Turning the tide – how to make changes when you're working with dinosaurs.'

3   Video: 'Accountants who win business by blogging – five ideas you can steal.'

You'll find a *Get to Know Your Customers* template in the Resources section at the back of the book to help you create buyer personas for your business.

Step 3 Pick the right mix of content creation and distribution tools

Now decide which tools to use to convey these messages and when to bring them in. With blogs, social media, newsletters video, webinars, e-books, info-graphics, etc you have a wide range of content options and formats to select from. The choice is down to you – it's about selecting the right mix of content-creation methods and distribution channels for your business and your clients or customers. The most important thing is to start sharing valuable content in earnest but you will find that a joined-up approach works best.

There are two different approaches you can take to get your valuable content marketing efforts off the ground. You either opt for the low risk 'Start Small and Grow' strategy or jump in feet first and 'Go Large and Repurpose'. Both routes are effective and eventually will get you to the same point.

The 'Start Small and Grow' approach to valuable content marketing

This is the lean, agile approach to valuable content marketing. Start your content flowing and add deeper, wider content as your confidence and trust in the approach grows. Find your feet then gradually build up the value you deliver to your audience over time for a deeper experience and better business results. Get au fait with each tool, master it and move on, like this:

Start creating and distributing your content

- *First, set up a **blog**.*
- *Engage in **social media**.*

How to tell if you are doing well: growing numbers of people reading and com-menting on your blog articles; growing numbers of followers on social media; more referrals and inbound enquiries; more sales.

Motivate more people to find you and engage with you

- *Start a monthly **email newsletter** and invite your contacts.*
- *Get more strategic with your blogging efforts. Learn what you need to about **search engine optimization**.*

How to tell if you are doing well: growth in your list of sign-ups to your newsletter; number of people who open and click on your newsletter and share your blog articles; more comments on your blog; improved search engine ranking for the keywords you have chosen; more inbound enquiries; more referrals; more sales.

Add deeper content

- *Write **deeper content**.*
- *Diversify with **different formats** – video, audio, graphic, dynamic tools.*

How to tell if you are doing well: number of people who download and share your content; more followers on social media; more sign-ups to your email list; more referrals; more PR opportunities; more inbound enquiries; more sales.

Widen your influence: take your content on tour

- *Write and post articles on **other websites**.*
- *Seek **speaker slots** to get your ideas out there.*

How to tell if you are doing well: your articles accepted on other well-recognized sites; PR and speaking opportunities coming to you; resulting in more followers, sign-ups, referrals, inbound leads and sales.

Do all this and you will build up a veritable library of valuable content that your customers will naturally gravitate towards, but don't rest on your laurels. Continue to grow and deepen the content experience for your contacts and customers, upping the value you deliver over time. The more you put in, the more you get out: your generosity and creativity will be rewarded.

The benefits of the 'Start Small and Grow' strategy:

1 An achievable, lower risk route to new marketing with valuable content.
2 Ability to test and prove the benefits as you go.
3 Advantage that benefits and confidence grow over time.

The alternative to 'Start Small and Grow' is a strategy that consumes more resources, but has definite strengths.

The 'Go Large and Repurpose' approach

There is a more ambitious valuable content starting strategy too: one that takes more upfront investment in terms of thought, resource, time and cost but will make a big impact and give you a library of content to share and repurpose straight away.

This is the 'Go Large and Repurpose' strategy. Companies that go down this route take a leap of faith and create some deep, stock content alongside the lighter stuff right from the start:

- They create a blog, newsletter and social media feeds.
- At the same time they create a valuable download, guide, research or valuable video.
- All of this is wrapped up in their valuable, lead-generating website, carefully designed to convert interest into action.

The 'Go Large and Repurpose' strategy takes longer to plan and implement but the benefit comes quickly in terms of increased credibility and exposure once your big body of content is circulating the web and the social networks. It takes more upfront investment but can save you time, money and effort in the long run. Once you are up and running the results happen very quickly. The real advantage of creating deeper content is that it can be repurposed (or 'atomized' as it is sometimes known). You can spin it into so many different formats and reuse it in many different ways: a valuable investment for the future and a benefit to your clients as they can then consume your content in any way they choose.

The thinking and writing that you do upfront for a deep piece of content can be stretched and tweaked in many directions, to fit the needs of different audiences and the styles of specific channels. This gives you a stock of great ideas to mine for content for the future, and saves you time going forward.

The 'Go Large and Repurpose' strategy is a powerful approach that really pays in terms of instant credibility and faster results. And it will give your sales team some seriously useful collateral to open doors and motivate new opportunities from the start, as you learned in Chapter 12.

Investing from the start in both stock and flow at Ascentor

Dave James is MD of Information Risk Management consultancy Ascentor. Mentioned throughout the book, Ascentor is a great example of a firm that has put valuable content at the heart of its marketing with impressive results.

Alongside redesigning the company website, setting up a blog and social media feeds Dave invested in the creation of some high-quality stock content from the start. Ascentor's valuable e-book: *The Board's Guide to Information Risk* and interactive online risk review tool take centre stage on their new website at launch. He explains:

The guide and the online information risk review are the centrepieces of a new valuable website. We knew we needed to make a big impact to make rapid inroads into a new market, so we opted to Go Large from the start.

Alongside our blog this heavyweight content gives our target clients and sales team a huge amount of useful information. Creating all this content took a lot of head scratching and a fair bit of investment in terms of editing and design too, but all our hard work is paying off.

Within a week of completing the guide it had helped us to land a new assignment and it is building a healthy pipeline of leads and sales.

www.ascentor.co.uk @ascentor

The 'Go Large and Repurpose' strategy has delivered swift results for Ascentor. Its web traffic doubled in the first month and within three months they were getting a stream of new enquiries from the web. Ascentor is on track to achieve its ambitious target of 40 per cent growth this year. Since the website launch, the company has been in active discussions with potential customers for business in excess of £400,000. Dave's company is set to achieve £2m turnover in the next financial year and has plans to employ two new people, as demand for their information security consultancy increases.

The benefits of the 'Go Large and Repurpose' strategy:

1 Instant impact.

2 Greater credibility and exposure from the start.

3 A library of great content to repurpose for the future.

Step 4 Make sure your website is up to the job

Whichever starting strategy you choose you'll need a solid web platform for all this valuable content. Will your current website do your new marketing strategy justice? Can you create or upload new content easily? Will people be able to find the valuable stuff on your site? Will your website convert their interest into action and motivate them to get in touch or stay in touch?

> *Even if you have stellar content such as e-books, webcasts, white papers, all roads ultimately lead back to your website. If your website is not resonating with prospects and clients, you are ultimately losing business.*
>
> Michele Linn, Savvy B2B Marketing @savvy_b2b

It could be time for a website redesign. If you understand how your content can be repurposed then the upfront investment in a stack of valuable content on your new website will become less of a 'nice to have, but can't afford' and more of a mandatory requirement in an integrated marketing strategy. Revisit the advice in Chapter 8.

Step 5 Plan like a publishing pro with a content calendar

Whether you 'Start Small' or 'Go Large', your aim is to work towards a bank of high-quality, valuable content that you can distribute throughout the year. Take time to plan this carefully. Work out your key content themes for the year and then plan the different types of content you will produce in these areas.

Here is what a year's worth of content looks like for Ascentor, the consultancy business we mentioned in the previous case study.

Quarter	Month	Activity						
		Social Media	LinkedIn	Blogs	Newsletter	Case studies	Discussion Papers	e-book
1	Jan	Every day	1-2 per week	●●				
	Feb			●●			●	
	Mar			●●		●		
2	Apr	Every day	1-2 per week	●●●	●			
	May			●●●	●		●	
	Jun			●●●	●	●		
3	Jul	Every day	1-2 per week	●●●	●			
	Aug			●●●	●		●	
	Sep			●●●	●	●		
4	Oct	Every day	1-2 per week	●●●	●			
	Nov			●●●	●			
	Dec			●●●	●	●		●

Setting your plan out like this helps you and the team maintain the discipline required for successful content marketing. If you don't plan in advance it is possible to get sidetracked, to get tied up in Tweeting and let the blogs slip, or to throw yourself into blog writing but not make time for those longer pieces of content.

Here are some things to think about when planning your content:

- **What content, when?** – a month by month plan, detailing the themes you are focusing on and showing clearly which pieces of content are needed when really helps.

- **Plan your themes** – the themes you are exploring with your longer pieces of content – the ebook and the white papers – will give a framework for your blogs. This avoids the 'what do I write about now?' problem that can arise if you just ask your team to start blogging.

- **Think ahead** – planning your themes in advance is a good use of time – you'll have them in mind as you write your short blogs, which makes turning your hand to a longer piece of writing less of a challenge.

- **Keep everyone on track** – once you've created your plan, share it with your team so that everyone knows exactly what is expected of them. A live calendar really helps here. People invariably get busy, and writing time can disappear if it's not pre-planned and safeguarded.

When you are planning your content think like a magazine editor. Plan your schedule and themes you want to talk about throughout the year. You can vary this as events arise – hot industry news, for example, that demands a fast response. The plan can flex but it really does help to start with a plan.

> ### Valuable Tip
>
> The best marketers link the content they create into the sales cycle. Think about the process your buyers go through to buy your product or services. Design appropriate content for every step – from the 'we've never heard of you before' stage to just about to buy.

Step 6 Put the right team together

To make this work you need a team and a budget. A commitment to valuable content means a new set of skills for many businesses. Customer research, design, SEO, social media, video production, email marketing, web development and mainly writing – there's a lot to learn and do. Up-skilling your team and doing as much as you can in-house makes economic sense but outsourcing is a valid option if you struggle to find the time, skills and resources to do it all yourselves. Outsourcing some activities will lessen the load.

Outsourcing vs insourcing for valuable content

	Advantages	**Disadvantages**
Producing valuable content in-house	Cost efficiencies Known quantity This is where the subject matter knowledge lies	May not have skills in-house Takes time Too close to the subject matter to give an independent view
Outsourcing valuable content production	Saves time – focus on core capabilities Specialist skills Independent, third party view	Higher cost Unknown quality Takes time to gain the specialist knowledge of the business

Hinge Marketing's study of online marketing in the professional services arena showed that almost a third of firms (31 per cent) outsource at least part of their online marketing functions (**www.hingemarketing.com**). In most cases, these firms are using a mixed model in which part of the online marketing is done in-house and part is outsourced. Help with writing or editing e-newsletters, blog posts, online articles, white papers and e-books was one of the most frequently outsourced functions.

Look for writers, content specialists or ex-journalists to help you create your content. As well as writing skills they will need insight, empathy and curiosity to ask the right questions, to understand and respond to your customers' issues and deliver your unique message. Specialist content consultancies and agencies like ours are new additions to the marketing services landscape, formed to deliver and coordinate the multiple tasks involved.

> *While you may cut media, printing, mailing, and call centre costs from your marketing budgets, plan to replace them with well-paid writers and analysts.*
>
> Christopher Butler author of The Strategic Web Designer **www.newfangled.com** @chrbutler

Given the direct impact of valuable content on growth and profitability, the costs of outsourcing can be justified.

Success with valuable content takes top team commitment and company-wide involvement, for it's the organization's knowledge that needs to be brought to the surface and turned into valuable content. Valuable content is a marketing approach that is too important to be left solely to the marketing department or your outsourced content partners. Your leaders, your experts, your technicians, your marketers, your customer service people, your sales team – these are the people whose expertise becomes content. You know your business and your clients and customers better than anybody and it is your ideas and your voice that need to shine through. Marketing the valuable content way gets much more of the company involved in business development – even those who didn't feel they had the 'sales and marketing skills' to participate in the traditional way.

> *I've been trying to get more people involved in the business development process for years! Creating and sharing valuable content has finally got the wider team engaged.*
>
> Nick Roberts, MD of The Landmark Practice

The companies that get the best payback from their efforts work hard to get a wide team engaged.

> *I went around and spoke to people about the new marketing approach, and told everyone that we all needed to write. I made sure that the impact on each person was low to start with – just one blog article per month from each department. It helps to share the load.*
>
> Nick Roberts, MD of The Landmark Practice **www.thelandmarkpractice.com** @tlpblog

Not everybody will find coming up with ideas and content easy but with the right encouragement and training you will unearth content stars in your business that shine through. These people can become skilled valuable content creators that others can learn from.

Valuable Tip

'If your in-house experts struggle to write then have someone else interview them to produce valuable content. The resulting documents should bear the name of both the writer and the expert. Sharing the credit doesn't diminish the reputations of your experts.'

Mel Lester **www.bizedge.biz** @mellester

Whether you do it in-house or outsource, someone in your business needs to take overall responsibility for telling your organization's story through the valuable content you share, and this person needs the support and commitment of the board. The US Content Marketing Institute (CMI) believes that every company should now employ what they call a Chief Content Officer.

> *The Chief Content Officer oversees all marketing content initiatives, both internal and external, across multiple platforms and formats to drive sales, engagement, retention, leads and positive customer behavior.*
>
> Joe Pulizzi, Content Marketing Institute **www.contentmarketinginstitute.com** @juntajoe

We back Joe Pulizzi's call. Valuable content is vital to the future of your business. It requires senior-level responsibility and skilled coordination to make it work.

Valuable Tip

Build your marketing department around the skills and processes needed to help the organization create and distribute high quality, valuable content.

Step 7 Measure, refine, learn and continue

You are ready to start creating all that content but before you press GO consider how you will know whether your new strategy is working. Revisit the objectives you set and put clear measures against each one to chart your progress towards your goals.

Example objectives and suggested measures

Business objectives	Indicators of progress
Greater awareness	Increase of followers on various social media platforms, website visitors, number of people who read your articles and other content.
More engagement	Number of downloads, sign-ups to your mailing list, opens of your email newsletters, shares on social media.
More inbound leads from the web	Number of leads related to your content.
More business	Number of opportunities motivated by your content that lead to sales.

Marketing on the web makes measurability so much easier. There are very effective free tools available to help you analyse the results of your investment in valuable content marketing:

- Google Analytics is the perfect place to start. Append a small piece of code to any web page and you can track how many people come to the page, what they do, where they are from and what they do next.

- Good blog software will show you how many visitors have read your blogs each day, which posts are popular and which not so much.

- Email marketing software gives you information on who has opened, clicked and acted on your email content.

- Social media tools give you frequent updates on who has shared your content or 'liked' your content, and how your follower list is growing.

- Link shorteners like bit.ly provide you with simple analytics on each content link you share (see: bitly.com).

The purpose of measurement is to check that you are going in the right direction. Stick a stake in the ground and look for indicators of progress. Tally the results up every month and chart against set goals. Measure the change.

Valuable Tip

Checking current statistics on Google Analytics or your latest e-newsletter is dangerously addictive, 'like crack cocaine' as one digital director recently commented. Remember to put more effort into creating your content than its vital statistics.

Today, you can measure lots of things. For example, where do you appear in search results? How many people are reaching out to you? How many people follow you on Twitter or like you on Facebook? The most important metric though, is 'How is business?' For companies that live and breathe how business is, you will see an immediate tie to growth and what you are doing online.

David Meerman Scott, author of The New Rules of PR and Marketing
www.webinknow.com @dmscott

David Meerman Scott sensibly advises you to keep a notepad and pen by the phone. With each new enquiry ask, '*How did you hear about us? What motivated you to get in contact?*' Keep a record of what they say. You'll probably find that their answers show a combination of factors – they might have heard of you from a contact, or found you on social media, checked out your websites and liked what they saw. Alternatively, they may have stumbled upon one of your blog articles via a Google search when looking for answers to an issue, liked what they saw but signed up to your email newsletter or Twitter feed to hear more. Valuable content marketing builds interest, trust and credibility in many ways.

You won't know what content is going to work best until you try it. You may think that an e-book will be the best thing ever, but, once you put your heart and soul into it, you find out that your audience seems to gravitate towards video instead. Be prepared to learn and adapt to audience needs. Measure your success and adjust for even more of it.

So take action and be patient. Marketing with valuable content is not a quick fix; it's a slow burn and it's worth the wait.

> *It took two months before the first leads from our new valuable content website started to come in. The head of steam built pretty quickly after that and we now get about 15 inbound leads from our site every week.*
>
> Paul Marsden, Director of Payplus The Payroll Service Centre
> **www.payroll-services-centre.co.uk** @payrollsc

Awareness and results from your valuable content marketing build over time. At the start it may feel like you are talking to yourself but hold the faith, focus on your customers and their needs, keep providing value, listen, learn, refine and success will come. Creating and sharing valuable content is the right thing to do.

Make it a habit: valuable for life.

CONCLUSION

YOUR NEW MARKETING MANIFESTO

We will focus our marketing on creating really valuable information for our customers

In the nine months it has taken us to write this book, we've seen more and more businesses realizing that they need to get to grips with the way they market their products and services. When we started we often had to explain what marketing with valuable content meant, but it is different today. Business owners now come to us to ask for help with their content, in the same way they might have asked for help with a brochure in the past. Our belief that to succeed you need to shift from simply selling to *seeking to be of value to your clients and customers* feels like part of a mainstream movement to find a better way to do business, and for that feels right.

We hope this book inspires you to put valuable content at the heart of your marketing, because we see what it does for those that adopt this thoughtful, client-centred joined up approach. Yes it will take work and commitment – it's not all simple – you'll need to take some risks, and probably make a few mistakes along the way (we have). Being valuable is not something you can pay lip service to, or tackle half-heartedly, but you have the tools and resources right here, and you can make it work. You have the most fantastic opportunity to build your business, starting right now. We hope you will seize it.

We'll leave you with a manifesto for your marketing…

…and a very important question to answer: **What information will your customers value?**

Be generous, get creative; we wish you the very best of luck.

ADDITIONAL RESOURCES

How valuable is your content now?

Take the valuable content test to pinpoint how useful your marketing really is today. This will help you to focus your efforts and improve your results.

1. **Our marketing activity generates good leads that drive sales.**

    a) Yes, most of the time.

    b) Sometimes, but we'd like more leads.

    c) No, not very often.

2. **We actively market our business online and get results.**

    a) Yes. We have a website that works for us and we spread our content across the web. 50 per cent of new business or more comes via the web.

    b) To an extent. We have a website but we don't do much else online. We'd like better results.

    c) No, we don't really market our business online yet.

3. **Potential customers welcome our marketing.**

    a) Yes. Our marketing is all about creating and sharing helpful, relevant and meaningful information and our customers tell us they appreciate it.

    b) Sometimes – sharing useful content is a small part of what we do.

    c) No, not often.

4. **We post fresh content on our website regularly.**

   a) Yes – twice a month or more.

   b) Occasionally.

   c) No, the content hardly ever changes.

5. **We have a working business blog.**

   a) Yes. We post a new article regularly and generate good leads from our blogging efforts.

   b) To an extent. We do have a blog. We post from time to time but don't really get much engagement or leads.

   c) No. We don't have a business blog.

6. **We engage in social media for business.**

   a) Yes. And it generates useful contacts, referrals and sales opportunities.

   b) A bit. We dabble. But it's not really generating any business results.

   c) No. We don't use social media yet.

7. **We make sure search engines can find our content.**

   a) Yes. Search Engine Optimization (SEO) is an important part of our strategy – we know the keywords we want to be found for and index our content carefully.

   b) A bit. We don't understand it fully yet.

   c) No. SEO is not part of our strategy.

8. **We have built an engaged list of contacts and keep in touch with a useful newsletter.**

   a) Yes. We send out a regular, valuable communication to our subscribed list of contacts.

   b) Kind of. We send out company news regularly but it's really a sales pitch.

   c) No. We don't keep in touch with a useful newsletter.

9. **We share deeper content on our website, eg useful guides, white papers, presentations, videos or e-books.**

   a) Yes. We've invested in some really high-quality, heavy-hitting content that's easy to find on our website.

   b) We could do. We have some good resources lying around the office but we haven't yet put them up on our website.

   c) No. We haven't created this deeper type of content yet.

10 **Our marketing efforts are targeted at a specific niche (or niches).**

   a) Yes. We know exactly what type of clients or customer we'd like to attract and we produce relevant information they connect with and value.

   b) To an extent, but it's a bit hit and hope.

   c) No. Our marketing is pretty scattergun. We think we might miss out on opportunities if we make it too specific.

Your score

Mostly a's. Congratulations! It sounds as if you are getting your marketing right with good results in terms of leads and sales. You evidently appreciate that regularly sharing valuable content will help you to build relationships with the kind of customers you seek. You'll find advanced tips throughout this book to make your content even more valuable. As a reward for your efforts please enter your website for a valuable content award: **www.valuablecontent.co.uk/ valuablecontentaward**

Mostly b's. You're on the right track but definitely room for improvement here. Get your content right and you'll see far better results from your online marketing in terms of leads and sales.

Mostly c's. All is not lost but you are definitely missing a trick with your marketing. If you want to get found on the web and continually generate good leads from your marketing efforts, with prospects coming to you, you really need this book! Read it and act on it to transform your content and win more business.

For an accurate score and personalized report for your business take the Valuable Content Test online on our website – **www.valuablecontent.co.uk**.

'Get to know your customers' template

This template will help you to get clear on who you are producing your content for and what content will really hit the mark. Answer the following questions to build a clear picture of your customers and their needs:

- What are you selling?
- What type of people can benefit from each service or product?
- Identify profitable groups in your target market that share common interests and concerns. Paint a picture of a dream customer in each group. These pictures are sometimes called 'buyer personas' and will help you keep your content on track. It helps to think of a real person. When it comes to your area of expertise, what's on his or her mind?
- What problems or challenges is this person trying to solve?
- How do they usually solve them?
- What are they trying to achieve? What's their goal?
- What are the common questions they would ask you or your sales team?
- What words or phrases do they use to describe the challenges they face?
- What phrases would they search on to find your products or services on the web?
- What is going on in the market? What are the big topics they'd be interested in?
- Where do they go for information? What organizations do they belong to?
- Think about what you can provide to meet their needs.
- What answers can you provide?
- What information would they appreciate at each stage of the buying process, from 'just looking' to 'just about to buy'?
- What content, in what format would meet their needs?

Describe your different target customers	What questions are they asking?	What answers can you provide?

No-nonsense glossary of SEO terms

anchor text   The text you include when you share a link in your site. Incorporate relevant keywords – the web page is then 'anchored' to this keyword, showing its importance to search engines.

heading tags   (H-tags) Tags (eg h1, h2, h3) used to label your headings and subheadings. These tags not only indicate the formatting for the heading but also allow search engines to recognize their importance (h1 tag in particular).

inbound links/backlinks   Links from an external web page to your web page.

indexing   Spiders index the content they find in a giant database, sorted according to how relevant it is to particular words that people use when they search.

keyword research   The process of collecting and analysing keywords to decide which ones you want to focus on for ranking your business website, web page or post to rank for.

keywords   Words or phrases that people type into a search engine to find relevant information. These keywords can be used for SEO purposes.

metadata   Data used to label your content to allow search engines to understand what your web page is all about. Three types of meta 'tags' that are important here:

- **meta title**   The title of a web page. The title tag is very important for SEO and often contains the keywords you want the web page to rank for.

- **meta description**   This is a <165-character summary of the content of a web page and is displayed below the blue link on a Google search results page.

- **meta keywords**   A list of keywords relevant to the web page.

offsite SEO   What you can do off your site in order to rank well for search engine search terms – eg building links from as many relevant external web sites as possible back to yours.

onsite SEO   What you can do on your site in order to rank for search engine search terms.

outbound links   Links from your web page to another web page (normally on an external site).

ranking   This is the order in which search engines deliver the results to search queries. It's controlled by highly complex, top-secret algorithmic functions. These functions basically determine whether your content or someone else's content best satisfies the search query. The higher you rank the more visitors you'll get.

search engine   Computer program (eg Google, Yahoo, Bing or a website search bar) designed to search for information on the whole web or within a particular website.

search engine optimization (SEO)   Stuff you do to your website so that it appears at the top of search engine results pages.

spiders or bots   A computer program that crawls around web pages, finding and updating information to index. They move around by following links from your page to other pages.

valuable content   Food for search engines, and where you need to focus your efforts on the web.

Checklist for your website content

Through answering the questions within the structure laid out below, this should help you pull together a file of information to build the content for your website. It should also allow you to get to the heart of your proposition and make sure the content of your site reflects your message accurately.

About us

What? In a nutshell, describe what you do.

Who? List the different types of company and people that benefit from your services.

Where? Where are your clients based?

Why? Explain why they need you – What issues do you solve for them?

Keywords – What would your clients search for online to find your services?

Specialism – What are your particular skills and expertise?

Company history – How long have you worked in this industry? When did you set up your company?

Quick company facts – What's the company structure, number of employees, etc? Describe the team.

Awards – List any awards, accolades or relevant qualifications/associations.

Ambition – Where would you like to see the business going?

Aims – What do you want from your communications and website?

Our approach

Motivation – What inspired you to set up in business? What was the idea behind it? What difference did you set out to achieve?

What does your company stand for? What do you believe in? What values are important to you?

Biggest frustration – What bugs you about your industry?

What do you most enjoy? What is the biggest kick you get out of work?

Approach – Describe your approach to your work.

Benefits – How does your approach make life easier for your customers?

Competitors – Who are your competitors?

Why choose you? What makes your approach different and better than all the other companies in your space?

Who/what inspires you?

Our services

Specialism – What are your particular skills, specialisms and expertise? What are you known for?

What do you do? – List and group your services.

Core services – Which are your most popular ones?

Useful structure for service copy – For each service, list the following:

- name of service;
- who this is relevant for;
- why they need it/what problem it solves;
- what your service involves;
- benefits;
- relevant image/photo/video;
- case studies;
- client testimonials, if any.

Our people

Staff details – List staff members, job titles and profiles for the team.

Photos – Provide professional photos of all staff (consistent style).

LinkedIn – Provide links to the staff's LinkedIn profiles.

Business personality – Any other information that conveys the human side to your business.

Valuable resources

Deeper written content, eg guides, handbooks, support information.

Different formats – Video or audio downloads?

Other useful information – What else would your clients find useful/ interesting? For example: FAQs, Jargon Buster, Online Assessment?

Additional information

Contact Us page – Contact details (and map).

Further features:

- company blog;
- sign up to mailing list or newsletter;
- search this site;
- client login area;
- press releases;
- in the news;
- downloadable documents;
- jobs;
- case studies;
- webcasts;
- social media links, eg to your Twitter account or LinkedIn profile;
- RSS feed;
- contact forms.

Questions to help you write a good case study

Every important project deserves a well-written case study. Use these questions and template to create valuable case studies as success stories for your website.

A. Questions for you

1. Client and project information

- Company name:
- Website address:
- Type of business:
- Client names/positions:
- Dates of project:
- Name of project:
- Type of project/service you delivered:
- Your expertise that you are looking to highlight with this case study:

2. Describe the challenge (for your client, not for you)

- What is your client's business and marketplace?
- Why did the client hire you? Describe their situation — what were they looking to achieve? What problems did they want you to solve for them? What were the business issues?
- What did they ask you to do?
- What would have happened if they had done nothing?
- What other approaches did they look at?
- What was it about your company or approach that they particularly liked?

3. Describe your solution to their problem

- What did you propose?
- What did you deliver? What was the service?
- What was unique or interesting about your approach? Describe any interesting methods/tools/technologies that you used.
- How was the client involved? Who did you work with? How long did it take?

4. Describe the results for the client

- How has the client benefited from your work? What were the immediate benefits? What are the longer-term benefits/what do you expect the longer-term benefits to be?
- How did the client feel about your work and the results achieved? What did he/she say?

5. Highlight your expertise

- What particular skills did you bring to bear on this project?
- What do you want this case study to demonstrate?
- What kind of client/company could benefit from this type of service?
- At what point would they pick up the phone to you?

6. Client quotes

- What has the client said about your work?
- What would you like the client to say about your work? If they asked you to write the quote for them, what would you say?

7. Design

- Do you have any images/pictures/design ideas to illustrate this example?
- Layout and style ideas?

8. Target audience

- Who is this case study written for? Who would you like to read it?
- What style of writing suits this audience – eg formal, conversational, technical, straightforward?

9. Learning points

- List things others customers or clients can learn from this experience.
- What valuable tips can they take away from this case study?

Actions:

Complete this overview in as much detail as you can. Then ask someone unrelated to the project to interview your client contact(s) and record their feedback on your work. Combining the information from both sources makes for a compelling case study.

B. Questions for your clients

The best case studies tell the client's story, not your own. The best way to do this is to involve the client in the writing of the case study. Before you put pen to paper, interview your client contacts. Ask them about the challenge they faced and why your solution was so helpful, what results they achieved. There's nothing like hearing it played back in the client's words.

Use these questions to get feedback from client contacts, to help create case studies for your website.

Hi. I'm conducting interviews for company X. You are a great success story. Can I ask you a few questions about the project?

- How did you initially come into contact with Company X?
- What challenge did you want their help with? What was your original objective?
- What other solutions did you consider to deliver this work?
- Why did you select Company X? What expertise did you hope they would bring?
- What solutions have they provided for you?
- What results have they delivered?
- What are the benefits to your company? What has this enabled you to do?
- How have you found dealing with Company X? Overall, have they done a good job?
- What advice can you offer them for similar projects in the future? What should they do more of, or less of, in your view?
- How do they compare with other suppliers you have worked with?
- Would you recommend Company X? For what types of project?
- If you had to describe Company X to a colleague what would you say?
- Is there anything else you want them to know?
- Thank you very much for your comments. Is there any other feedback you'd like to give? Anything else you'd like to say?

Planning questions for deeper written content

Creating high-quality papers, guides and e-books takes more time and thought than writing a blog article but it is well worth the extra effort in terms of the credibility these bestow.

Before you start writing, plan your paper carefully. If you put effort into the planning it will make the paper far easier to write, with less rework through the process and a high quality more engaging paper as a result. Here are some questions to help you.

Answer these questions before you start to write:

1. Working title and subtitle?

The title matters. Keep it short, reader-focused, engaging and active. Add a subtitle to set the context.

2. Purpose?

Why are you writing this paper? What is your overall objective? Start with the end game in sight: what do you want it to do for your business?

3. Target reader?

Who are you writing this for? Describe your typical reader. What business are they in? What role do they hold? What frustrates them? Why do they need this paper?

4. Content?

- What is it all about? What questions does it answer? What issues does it solve?
- Why is it important? What is happening in the market that makes this subject important?
- What are your main messages? What will the reader learn from it?
- Headings and ideas for main sections?
- Any case studies/research/testimonials to back up your approach? (Give links)

5. Style?

- Tone: formal, personal?
- Design: what do you want it to look like/not look like?
- Suggested illustrations, diagrams, images?
- Length?

6. Search engines?

Make sure your content gets found. What keywords or phrases would people search on to find this paper?

7. Summary?

Summarize the paper for the reader.

Quoted experts and recommended reading

Books

Google+ for Business: How Google's social network changes everything, Chris Brogan, Que, 2011

The Go-Giver: A little story about a powerful business idea, Bob Burg and John David Mann, Penguin Books, 2010

Spiraling Up: How to create a high growth, high value professional services firm, Lee W Frederiksen and Aaron E Taylor, Hinge Research Institute, 2010

The Trusted Advisor Fieldbook: A comprehensive toolkit for leading with trust, Charles H Green and Andrea P Howe, Wiley, 2012

Trust-based Selling: Using customer focus and collaboration to build long-term relationships, Charles H Green, McGraw Hill, 2006

Inbound Marketing: Get found using google, social media and blogs, Brian Halligan and Dharmesh Shah, Wiley, 2010

Content Rules: How to create killer blogs, podcasts, videos, ebooks, webinars (and more) that engage customers and ignite your business, Ann Handley and C C Chapman, Wiley, 2011

Stories that Sell: Turn satisfied customers into your most powerful sales and marketing asset, Casey Hibbard, AIM Publishers, 2009

Duct Tape Marketing: The world's most practical small business marketing guide, John Jantsch, Thomas Nelson Publishers, 2006

The Trusted Advisor, David H Maister, Charles H Green, and Robert M Galford, Simon & Schuster, 2002

Perfect Presentations, Andrew Leigh and Michael Maynard, Random House Books, 2009

Making Change Happen: A practical guide to implementing business change, Jane Northcote, 2008

A Website That Works: How marketing agencies can create business generating sites, Mark O'Brien, Rockbench Publishing, 2011

Managing Content Marketing: The real-world guide for creating passionate subscribers to your brand, Robert Rose and Joe Pulizzi, CMI Books, 2011

The New Rules of Marketing & PR: How to use news releases, blogs, podcasting, viral marketing & online media to reach buyers directly, 3rd edn, David Meerman Scott, Wiley, 2011

Watertight Marketing, Bryony Thomas, Ecademy, 2012

Principled Selling: How to win more business without selling your soul, David Tovey, Kogan Page, 2012

The Financial Times Guide to Business Networking: How to use the power of online and offline networking for business success, Heather Townsend, Pearson Education Ltd, 2011

Writing White Papers: How to capture readers and keep them engaged, Michael A Stelzner, WhitePaperSource Publishing, 2007

UnMarketing: Stop marketing, start engaging, Scott Stratten, Wiley, 2010

The Corporate Blogging Book, Debbie Weil, WordBiz.com, 2010

Valuable websites to be inspired by

Hinge Marketing: www.hingemarketing.com

Trusted Advisor: trustedadvisor.com

Newfangled: www.newfangled.com

Balsamiq: www.balsamiq.com

Recourses: www.recourses.com

Intel's Inside Scoop: scoop.intel.com

Ascentor: www.ascentor.co.uk

HSBC Expat site: www.expat.hsbc.com

Mackay Flooring: www.mckayflooring.co.uk

Indium Corporation: www.indium.com

Base Structures: www.basestructures.com

See our valuable content award winners for more examples: www.valuablecontent.co.uk/valuable-content-award

Business development blogs to learn from

Principled Selling: www.principledselling.org

Copyblogger: www.copyblogger.com

Clear Thought marketing blog: www.clear-thought.co.uk/in_thought

Web Ink Now: www.webinknow.com

Jim's Marketing Blog: jimsmarketingblog.com

Trusted Advisor: trustedadvisor.com/trustmatters

Newfangled blog: www.newfangled.com/newfangled_employee_blogs

Hinge Marketing blog: www.hingemarketing.com/blog

MarketingProfs: www.marketingprofs.com

Jim O'Connor's Stories That Sell blog: blog.storiesthatsell.co.uk

Ian Brodie: www.ianbrodie.com

Chris Pearson's Thesis blog: www.pearsonified.com

Su Butcher's blog: www.justprofessionals.net

Iain Claridge's design blog: www.iainclaridge.co.uk/blog

Acknowledgements

Although we have helped others to make their books happen there is nothing like going through the experience yourself to make you really understand. Now we know why the acknowledgements page is so important! A book is a massive collaboration. It would have been impossible to do this alone, and far less interesting. So here we go. Without trying to make it sound like an acceptance speech at the Oscars we are extremely grateful to:

- Liz Gooster and our publishing team at Kogan Page – for your belief and encouragement.
- Robert Watson, our editor in Australia – for your clear direction, detailed edits, late-night Skype calls and unerring patience.
- Lizzie Everard – for the beautiful illustrations. Your ability to make our ideas visual gave us new angles on the text. Lizzie – your designs make us very happy.
- Claire Rosling – for all that calm, intelligent support. We've loved working with you and wish you all the best with your environmental career.
- Ruth Cox – for your words of wisdom on the publishing industry, for making us laugh and keeping us on track.
- Eli Barbary and Toby Duckett – for being there to pick up the pieces and ensure our own valuable content continues to flow.
- Reviewers Bill Maryon, Adrian Knight, Anna Wilson, Bryony Thomas, Lucinda Brook, James Perrott and James Jefferson.

- Lally and Richard Temple-Cox for lending us your gorgeous house in Aberdovey for a few days of quiet writing and a stunning view.
- The fantastic community of freelance businesses here at Spike Design, Spike Island, and the many cups of tea, chocolate biscuits and kind words that you have sent our way.

We'd like to thank all the experts who have contributed tips and stories and inspiration for this book – Charles H Green and Andrea Howe, Bryony Thomas, David Tovey, Richard Wylie and the team at Questas, Lee Duncan, Heather Townsend, David Meerman Scott, Adrian Knight of Digital Investments, Jane Northcote, Peldi at Balsamiq, Jim O'Connor, Iain Claridge, Paul Simister, Stephen King at F-works, David Gilroy of Conscious Solutions, Mick Dickinson, Ian Brodie, the team at Hinge Marketing, Chris and Mark at Newfangled, Michael Maynard at Maynard Leigh, Teresa Harris, Dan Roberts, Roland Millward, Simon Murie of Swimtrek, the team at Endurance Life, Tony Restell of Top Consultant, Paul Marsden of Payplus, Julian Summerhayes, Bob Burg, Lucinda Brook, Mark Sinclair of yourBusinessChannel, James Chapman, Su Butcher, Matthew Curry, Jay and Ali at Yoke Design, David Nutley, Brian Inkster, Jim Connolly, Ann-Marie McCormack, Louise-Barnes Johnstone, Richard Dennys, and the team at HSBC expat. What a list! You have our respect and our thanks.

We are also grateful to our clients who have trusted us to help them with their businesses: to Ascentor, The Landmark Practice, The Payroll Services Centre, F-Works, Formicio, Development Done Right and RSG. You have been a pleasure to work with. A quick shout out to our Twitter communities who have sent notes of encouragement in 140 characters or less!

And finally a huge thank you to our families, to our supportive and long-suffering partners JJ and Bill and our fantastic kids for putting up with absent, distracted mothers over the months it took to write this book. We hope to make you all proud.

And that does sound very much like an Oscar acceptance speech!

Sonja and Sharon

INDEX